REVISED AND UPDATED

THE BEST
Veggie Burgers
★ ON THE PLANET ★

Just Got Better!

THE BEST
Veggie Burgers
★ ON THE PLANET ★

Just Got Better!

More than 100 Plant-Based Recipes
for Vegan Burgers, Fries,
and More

JONI MARIE NEWMAN

FAIR WINDS

Inspiring | Educating | Creating | Entertaining

Brimming with creative inspiration, how-to projects, and useful information to enrich your everyday life, Quarto Knows is a favorite destination for those pursuing their interests and passions. Visit our site and dig deeper with our books into your area of interest: Quarto Creates, Quarto Cooks, Quarto Homes, Quarto Lives, Quarto Drives, Quarto Explores, Quarto Gifts, or Quarto Kids.

© 2019 Quarto Publishing Group USA Inc.
Text © 2011, 2019 Joni Marie Newman

First Published in 2019 by Fair Winds Press, an imprint of The Quarto Group,
100 Cummings Center, Suite 265-D, Beverly, MA 01915, USA.
T (978) 282-9590 F (978) 283-2742 QuartoKnows.com

Fair Winds Press titles are also available at discount for retail, wholesale, promotional, and bulk purchase. For details, contact the Special Sales Manager by email at specialsales@quarto.com or by mail at The Quarto Group, Attn: Special Sales Manager, 100 Cummings Center, Suite 265-D, Beverly, MA 01915, USA.

23 22 21 20 19 2 3 4 5

ISBN-13: 978-1-59233-884-9

Digital edition published in 2019
eISBN-13: 978-1-63159-740-4

Originally found under the following Library of Congress Cataloging-in-Publication Data

Newman, Joni-Marie.
101 globally inspired vegan creations packed with fresh flavors and exciting new tastes / Joni Marie Newman ; with photography by Celine Steen.
   p. cm.
Includes index.
ISBN-13: 978-1-59233-476-6
ISBN-10: 1-59233-476-8
1. Meat substitutes. 2. Hamburgers. 3. Vegan cooking. 4. Cookbooks. I. Title. II. Title: One hundred one globally inspired vegan creations packed with fresh flavors and exciting new tastes. III. Title: One hundred and one globally inspired vegan creations packed with fresh flavors and exciting new tastes.
TX838.N485 2011

641.5'636--dc22   2010049438

Cover and book design: Laura Klynstra
Photography: Celine Steen and Kate Lewis (cover and title page)

Photography on pages [6, 10, 16, 32, 52, 66, 78, 96, 112, 136, 156, 174, 186, 204, 214]: www.thinkstock.com

Printed and bound in China

This book is for Nolan, Dominic, Alayna, Evelyn, Olivia, and Phoenix. The older you get, the more I love you! Continue to grow into the beautiful people I know your parents have taught and are still teaching you to be.

xoxo, *Aunt Joni*

Contents

Introduction

You are about to embark on a culinary journey that will test your standard knowledge of ingredients and their form, function, and texture. Foods that you thought should be eaten with a fork or spoon have been transformed into round, handheld patties of goodness that serve up most perfectly between two pieces of bread.

A lot has changed in the world of veggie burgers in the decade since this book was first published. I have watched, firsthand, the changing of the burger guard. Tremendous progress has been made in commercially available veggie burgers — ones that are indistinguishable from their cow-flesh counterparts. Some of them even "bleed!" Controversy aside, no more do we have to suffer the hockey-puck-like frozen discs of funky colored vegetable mash masquerading as a burger smelling faintly like a cross between cooked carrots and liquid smoke. No!

Now we have amazing fresh patties like Beyond Meat's Beyond Burger, and Impossible Foods' Impossible Burger, being served up in fast food as well as fine dining establishments. We can buy chubs of vegan ground beef from Lightlife Foods or Tofurky if we want to form our own patties. We can pick up a pack of Gardein Ultimate Beefless Burgers, or Don Lee Farm's "bleeding" Plant-Based Burgers, to throw in the freezer to have on hand whenever we want a tasty burger.

The store-bought and restaurant offerings are just so great now, I actually thought twice about rewriting this book! But then a little voice spoke to me. People LOVE to make their own veggie burgers from scratch. People love to cook and create in the kitchen. And goodness knows, I have grown a lot in the last ten years, both in my approach to scratch cooking, and in my methods. New ingredients and new techniques are always inspiring new ideas. It's been a decade of change, and this book was just waiting to be updated. So, here it is! *The Best Veggie Burgers on the Planet* . . . just got better!

Know this: I have presented you with 101 burgers. But these need not be the limit to your burger concoctions and creations. Be inspired to get into the kitchen and create. Look at those same old ingredients in a whole new way. Anything can become a burger. Anything.

Now, go forth and create a tasty burger!

Chapter 1

HOW TO
USE THIS
BOOK

Tips, Tricks, and Troubleshooting

Throughout this book you will note that some recipes are listed as soy- or gluten-free. I have taken care to make sure that these recipes do not include the major offenders, but, please, if you have food allergies, or are on a restricted diet, double-check ingredients, especially vinegars, flavor extracts, soy sauces, and other store-bought items.

Look for the following icons as you flip through the book:

Soy-Free   Nut Free   Gluten-Free   No-Oil Added   No-Sugar Added

You will also notice the use of the terms *sour cream, milk, yogurt, butter, cheese,* and so on. I am sure you already know this, but when mentioned, I mean the nondairy, vegan versions of these ingredients.

One word you will find often in the directions is *dough*. I refer to the mass that forms when you mash all the burger-making ingredients into a patty-able consistency akin to dough. I know this term is usually reserved for baking recipes, but it seems to work efficiently here.

TIPS FOR KNEADING THE "DOUGH"

- I use my hands. Yes, it's messy, but I find that it gets the job done best. It also ensures that all of the ingredients are well incorporated. In addition, you can feel when the dough is the right consistency. It is easy to tell if you need to add more liquid or dry ingredients using this method.

TIPS FOR SHAPING YOUR PATTIES

- Use a cookie cutter! Find a round cookie cutter about 4 inches (10 cm) in diameter to form your burgers.

- Press the dough into the cookie cutter to desired thickness and pop out for perfectly round patties.

- For tofu, use the cookie cutter to cut the rounds directly from a slab of tofu.

TIPS FOR FREEZING AND REFRIGERATING

- By refrigerating the dough before forming your patties, you are allowing it to stiffen up, making it easier to form. This step is essential when working with gluten-based recipes, because it allows the wheat protein to "rest" and form the stringy texture that helps bind the burgers together.

- To freeze, place the patties in a single layer on a baking sheet. Place in the freezer. Once frozen, pluck 'em off the baking sheet and place in a resealable plastic bag and store in the freezer until needed. Or, place a small sheet of waxed paper between each patty and stack. Place the stack in a resealable plastic bag and store in the freezer until needed.

- There is no need to defrost the patties before cooking. Just plop 'em in a frying pan with a little oil, or bake, grill, or whatever! In fact, it has been my experience, as well as that of a tester or two, that frozen patties cook up better than fresh! They also tend to hold together better.

TIPS FOR RECONSTITUTING TEXTURED VEGETABLE PROTEIN (TVP)

- When microwaving, use plastic wrap to tightly cover your bowl or container. Don't ask me why, but this makes a world of difference, something about how it expands and contracts with the steam.

- If microwaving plastic wrap freaks you out, then you can bring liquid to a boil, pour it over the TVP granules, cover tightly, and let stand for 10 minutes.
- Use 1 cup (235 ml) of liquid per 1 cup (96 g) of TVP when reconstituting, unless otherwise noted.
- Use vegetable broth instead of water for more flavorful TVP.
- You can reconstitute a large batch of TVP all at once, and then store in an airtight container in the fridge. It should keep for up to a week.

TIPS FOR COOKING

Many veggie burgers are pretty much already cooked. When you bake, fry, or grill them, you are really just heating them up and giving them a little crust. Here are some of your options.

BAKING: If you have a Silpat, a silicone baking sheet, or parchment paper, use it! It works better than cooking spray, helps prevent burnt bottoms, and makes cleanup a snap.

When baking, cover your baking sheet or pan with a foil tent (essentially, a steam tent) to help retain moisture.

Most of the burgers can be baked at 350°F (180°C, or gas mark 4) for about 15 minutes per side.

FRYING: I almost exclusively use a cast-iron skillet. That way, I don't have to use too much oil. I preheat the oil in the pan before I add my patties.

I have found that when cooking unfrozen patties, it can take anywhere from 3 to 5 minutes per side over medium-high heat to get a good, golden crispy burger.

I use many types of oil—canola, grapeseed, extra-virgin olive, peanut, sesame—depending on the genre of the burger. Nonstick cooking spray is a good, low-calorie alternative to oil when frying up a burger. There are other burgers that benefit greatly from a "bake first, then fry" method.

AIR-FRYING: If you have an Air-Fryer, you can generally use 375°F (190°C) for anywhere from 12 to 18 minutes. Check out the handy Air-Fryer conversion calculator at www.airfryercalculator.com to help make your conversions easier.

GRILLING: Oil the grill, if possible. This will prevent sticking. Also rub a little oil on both sides of the burger before grilling; it will help you achieve those sought-after grill marks and help prevent sticking.

I like to pick a really hot part of the grill, throw on an oiled frozen patty, let it sit for 3 to 5 minutes on each side, and that's it.

Certain burgers don't hold up that well on the grill, so I use the "steam in foil" method. Loosely wrap the burger in foil and throw it on a not-too-hot portion of the grill and let it steam for 10 to 15 minutes, longer if frozen. You won't get the grill marks, but your burger should remain in one piece. For a little added "juice" you can brush the patty with some olive oil or your favorite flavored oil before steaming on the grill.

INGREDIENTS

Some of the ingredients used in this book may be new to you. Here is a short list and brief description of a few key ingredients.

BEANS: Out of convenience (and admittedly, laziness!) I like to use canned beans, rinsing and draining them thoroughly to get rid of unnecessary extra sodium. If you cook your own, more power to you! Keep in mind that one 15-ounce (425 g) can of beans generally equals approximately 1$2/3$ cups (294 g) cooked beans, or $2/3$ cup (120 g) dry beans.

FLOURS: For the sake of accuracy in measurements, I use a scoop to transfer flour into the measuring cup, so as not to over pack it. It can make a difference in how recipes turn out, so it's a good thing to keep in mind. I choose the flour based on the flavor profile of the burger. In general, you can substitute most flours based on what you have on hand, but be sure to pay attention to the consistency of your dough.

JACKFRUIT: A tropical fruit that can grow as big as 120 pounds (54 K)! The ripe fruit is sweet and tastes like a cross between a banana and a pineapple. In this book, I call for unripened "Young Green" jackfruit in cans. Make sure to pick up cans packed in water or brine, and not syrup. The fruit itself, when cooked, mimics shredded meats and has very little flavor on its own.

LIQUID SMOKE: This flavoring is stocked near the marinades in most markets. It's actually made by condensing smoke into liquid form. A little goes a long way in giving a smoky flavor to many foods.

NONDAIRY MILKS: I most commonly use soymilk, almond milk, or coconut milk when cooking. They seem to have the best results. However, if you have a preference for another type of milk, I am sure it will work just fine. I do recommend using soymilk in recipes when a "buttermilk" texture is needed.

NUTRITIONAL YEAST: This is the magical, nonactive kind of yeast most vegans adore. Its nutty, cheesy flavor makes it an indispensable ingredient in my pantry. Look for the vegetarian-support formula (this will be noted on the label), which is enriched with vitamin B12.

SALT AND PEPPER: I respect your habits when it comes to salt and pepper, so the measurements you will find in my recipes are meant as a guide. I usually add *to taste* so that you can follow your needs and preferences. I prefer using sea salt, because it retains a minuscule amount of minerals. And I like to use a small amount of black salt in recipes that replicate eggs, because it lends a delicate, sulfurous flavor to foods.

SEAWEED, SUCH AS HIJIKI, DULSE, AND NORI: Edible seaweeds add a fishy flavor to foods without using fish.

SOY SAUCE: This condiment can be replaced with tamari or Bragg Liquid Aminos. If you're watchful of your sodium intake, purchase the reduced-sodium kind. The liquid aminos only contains a small amount of natural sodium and happens to be gluten-free.

SRIRACHA OR "ROOSTER SAUCE": Made from chile peppers, garlic, vinegar, and salt ground together to form a smooth paste, this hot sauce is addictive. Check for ingredients, because some brands contain fish sauce.

SUGAR: I do not use refined white sugar. What I commonly refer to as *sugar* is almost always evaporated cane juice. Most refined white sugar is processed using charred animal bones. I prefer to keep the bones out of my sugar, so I stick with the more natural, cruelty-free versions.

TEMPEH: Tempeh is made from fermented soybeans pressed into a cake. Bitter to some, this whole-bean soy treat is a very versatile protein. Still afraid? Simmer tempeh in water or vegetable broth for about 20 minutes prior to using in recipes. It mellows the flavor.

TOFU: There are a few different types and textures out there. Soft silken tofu is best used for sauces and blended desserts, while it's best to use super firm (if you can find it, it is a huge time saver, because it requires very little, if any, pressing) or extra firm, and press before using. To press tofu, simply lay drained tofu on a clean folded kitchen towel. Place another clean towel on top and then top with a heavy skillet or book to press excess moisture out of the tofu.

TVP (Textured Vegetable Protein): This high protein, low fat ingredient is made from defatted soybeans. The oil is extruded from the bean, leaving behind a malleable mass that can be formed into shapes and dehydrated. This makes it shelf-stable and the perfect meat substitute to have on hand in your pantry. It's available in many forms, like chunks, granules, and strips. However, for the purposes of this book, I will always call for granules.

VITAL WHEAT GLUTEN FLOUR: Gluten is the natural protein portion removed from whole wheat. Vital wheat gluten flour can be found in most grocery stores or ordered online. It is important to know that vital wheat gluten flour is completely different from high gluten flour. The two are not interchangeable and will not perform similarly in recipes.

Chapter 2

BURGERS FOR BREAKFAST

*Can YOU think of a better
way to start the day?*

DENVER OMELET BURGER

Gluten-Free

No-Sugar Added

Nut-Free

This burger makes such a great, hearty breakfast with all the flavors you remember and love from a traditional Denver Omelet. Serve up warm topped with some salsa or Nondairy Sour Cream (page 198) on a toasted English muffin or bagel with some home fries or hash browns.

12 ounces (340 g) extra-firm tofu, drained and pressed

½ cup (120 ml) plus 2 tablespoons (30 ml) mild-flavored vegetable oil, divided, plus more for frying

1 teaspoon garlic powder

1 teaspoon onion powder

1 teaspoon mustard powder

½ teaspoon cumin

¼ teaspoon turmeric

¼ teaspoon paprika

1 cup (160 g) diced onion

1 red bell pepper, cored, seeded, and diced

1 green bell pepper, cored, seeded, and diced

⅛ teaspoon salt

¼ cup (25 g) imitation bacon bits, store-bought or homemade (page 201)

½ teaspoon liquid smoke

1 cup (120 g) chickpea (garbanzo) flour

YIELD: 6 BURGERS

In a blender, combine the tofu, ½ cup (120 ml) oil, garlic powder, onion powder, mustard powder, cumin, turmeric, and paprika, and process until smooth. Transfer to a mixing bowl and set aside.

Preheat the 2 tablespoons (30 ml) oil in a frying pan. Add the onion, bell peppers, and salt. Sauté until just beginning to brown. Remove from the heat and add to the tofu mixture.

Fold in the bacon bits and liquid smoke.

Add the chickpea flour and mix. The mixture is wet and sticky, but you should be able to form it into 6 patties.

Preheat plenty of oil in a frying pan and panfry for about 4 to 5 minutes per side, or until golden and crispy. Alternatively, rub each patty with a small amount of oil, and use your Air-Fryer at 375°F (190°C) for anywhere from 14 to 16 minutes.

You Are SO Vegan!

Skip the bacon bits and fold in finely chopped kale instead!

FRIED EGG TOFU BURGER

Gluten-Free *No-Oil Added* *No-Sugar Added* *Nut Free*

This perfectly round, bright yellow breakfast patty not only tastes like eggs, but packs a mean protein punch at the same time. Serve on a toasted English muffin, bagel, or bun with a slice of your favorite vegan cheese for an "Egg McMuffin" type of breakfast sandwich. Make sure to use a gluten-free bagel or bun when serving to keep it truly gluten-free.

1 pound (454 g) super or extra firm tofu, drained and pressed

½ cup (120 ml) water

2 tablespoons (15 g) nutritional yeast

1 teaspoon Dijon mustard

½ teaspoon turmeric

½ teaspoon garlic powder

½ teaspoon onion powder

¼ teaspoon salt

¼ teaspoon black pepper

Kala Namak (black salt), to taste

YIELD: 4 BURGERS

Carefully cut the block of tofu into slabs about ¼-inch (6-mm) thick. Using a 4-inch (10-cm) cookie cutter, cut four rounds from the slabs. Set aside.

Add remaining ingredients, except Kala Namak, to a resealable bag, or shallow dish with a lid, and mix well. Add tofu rounds to the mixture and marinate for at least 30 minutes, or up to overnight.

This patty can be cooked in several ways, my favorite being in the waffle iron! Add to the center of the waffle iron and close. Cook for 5 minutes, or until crisp and golden on the outside. This patty can also be baked at 350°F (180°C) for 10 minutes per side, Air-Fried for 12 minutes at 375°F (190°C), or pan-fried in a smidge of oil, over medium-high heat for about 3 minutes per side.

Once cooked, remove from heat and sprinkle with a pinch of Kala Namak for that extra egg-y flavor.

You Are SO Vegan!

Instead of a bun, opt to serve on a bed of wilted arugula with slices of juicy heirloom tomato.

GARLICKY RANCH POTATO BURGER

Soy-Free

No-Sugar Added

Nut Free

These are carb-o-licious. If you are looking for a low-carb or low-cal burger, then don't make these. They work well for breakfast, lunch, or dinner. Furthermore, they don't even need a bun! Just a schmear of good old-fashioned ketchup. If you're having them for breakfast, serve with a nice tofu scramble. For lunch or dinner, serve with a leafy green vegetable to balance out the carb overload. Or just go crazy and serve with a nice side of Garlicky Roasted Reds (see You Are SO Vegan, below) and run a marathon the next day.

2 cups (220 g) shredded russet potatoes (tightly packed), rinsed in cool water and drained to prevent discoloring

2 tablespoons (30 g) minced garlic

1 tablespoon (2 g) dried parsley or 3 tablespoons (12 g) chopped fresh parsley

1 teaspoon paprika

Salt and pepper

1 cup (115 g) panko bread crumbs

½ cup (62 g) all-purpose flour

2 tablespoons (13 g) ground flaxseed mixed with 3 tablespoons (45 ml) water

⅓ cup (80 ml) canola oil, plus extra for frying

YIELD: 4 TO 6 BURGERS

In a large bowl, combine the potatoes, garlic, parsley, paprika, and salt and pepper to taste. Mix until all of the potatoes are well coated.

Add the panko, flour, flax mixture, and ⅓ cup (80 ml) oil. Mix well, using your hands, until a nice dough forms.

Divide into 4 to 6 equal pieces and form into patties. The thinner your patty, the crispier it will be.

Preheat a generous amount of oil in a skillet and panfry for 3 to 5 minutes per side, or until golden and crispy.

You Are SO Vegan!

To make Garlicky Roasted Reds to serve alongside these burgers, first cut up a bag of baby red potatoes into bite-size chunks. Spread them in a single layer on a foil-lined baking sheet, with the skins down, and sprinkle with salt, pepper, paprika, garlic powder, parsley, and fresh minced garlic. Then drizzle a bit of olive oil over the whole thing and bake at 350°F (180°C, or gas mark 4) for about 30 minutes.

BACON AND EGG BREAKFAST BURGER

Nut Free

No-Sugar Added

Cruelty free bacon and tofu eggs go together like peanut butter and jelly in this burger that knocks the socks off any fast food breakfast sammy. When you're on the go, eat this on a whole wheat bun, an English muffin, or Bagel Bun (page 212), with a slice of vegan cheese or a little vegan garlic mayo. At home you can add a side of hash browns or home fries. Garnish with your favorite breakfast toppings (think omelet here: diced and grilled peppers and onions, salsa, ketchup, avocado, or spinach).

12 ounces (340 g) extra-firm tofu, drained and pressed

¼ teaspoon turmeric

1 tablespoon (8 g) garlic powder

1 tablespoon (8 g) onion powder

1 tablespoon (15 g) yellow mustard

¼ teaspoon sea salt

¼ cup (25 g) imitation bacon bits, store-bought or homemade (page 201)

½ to 1 cup (62 to 125 g) all-purpose flour

2 tablespoons (30 ml) oil, for frying

YIELD: 4 BURGERS

Crumble the tofu into a large mixing bowl.

Add the turmeric, garlic powder, onion powder, mustard, salt, and bacon bits, and stir to combine.

Knead in the flour a little at a time. Depending on how much moisture was left in your tofu, you may need a little or a lot. Knead the heck out of this until you get a nice ball of dough, at least 5 minutes.

Let sit for at least 15 minutes to rest. Divide the dough into 4 equal parts and form into patties.

Panfry in the oil for 4 to 5 minutes per side, or until nice and golden brown.

You Are SO Vegan!

Skip the bun and wrap this baby up in a giant leaf of collard greens or Swiss chard.

QUICHE LORRAINE BURGER

Delicieux pour le déjeuner ou à n'importe quel moment! Say what you will about the French, they know how to cook. Bon appetit! If you didn't quite get the translation, these are delicious for breakfast or anytime! Serve on a gluten-free bagel or toast, alongside some breakfast favorites, such as hash browns, and if you are really hungry, a nice tofu scramble. I also like to put a dollop of ketchup on mine.

Gluten-Free

Nut Free

No-Sugar Added

1 cup (120 g) chickpea flour

8 ounces (227 g) plain soy tempeh, crumbled

½ cup (50 g) imitation bacon bits, store-bought or homemade (page 201)

½ cup (60 g) nutritional yeast

¼ cup (72 g) white or yellow miso

¼ cup (60 g) nondairy cream cheese

1 teaspoon Kala Namak (black salt)

Oil, for frying

YIELD: 4 BURGERS

In a large mixing bowl, knead all the ingredients together into a thick mass. Really get in there with your hands and mash it together. There is not a lot of moisture in the mixture, so you have to use a little elbow grease. It'll come together.

Form into 4 patties.

Panfry in oil for 3 to 5 minutes per side, or until a nice golden crispy crust forms. Alternatively, use your Air-Fryer at 375°F (190°C) for 14 to 16 minutes.

You Are SO Vegan!

Tempeh timid? Don't be afraid of the fermented good stuff. If you are new to tempeh, try simmering it in water or broth for about 20 minutes before using it in recipes to mellow the fermented flavor.

LOG CABIN BURGER

The marriage of sweet and savory was the inspiration for this burger. This is my idea of a pancake mixed together with a sausage, all in one little package. To pull out the savory flavors, add a dollop of ketchup and eat it on its own, or sandwich the burger inside a homemade Bagel Bun (page 212) or Rustica Bun (page 209). To pull out the sweet flavors, serve on its own topped with a dollop of nondairy butter and some pure maple syrup. Served with a nice tofu scramble, this makes a very hearty breakfast.

8 ounces (225 g) plain soy tempeh

1 cup (125 g) all-purpose flour

⅓ cup (80 ml) pure maple syrup

¼ cup (56 g) nondairy butter

2 tablespoons (32 g) peanut butter

1 tablespoon (8 g) vegetable broth powder or ½ bouillon cube, crumbled

1 teaspoon liquid smoke

⅛ teaspoon paprika

Salt and pepper

Oil, for frying (optional)

—————

YIELD: 4 BURGERS

In a mixing bowl, crumble the tempeh into the smallest bits possible. Add the flour, maple syrup, butter, peanut butter, vegetable broth powder, liquid smoke, paprika, and salt and pepper to taste. Mix well, using your hands, until a nice dough forms.

Divide into 4 equal pieces and form into patties.

Cook as desired. Bake at 350°F (180°C, or gas mark 4) for 30 minutes, covered loosely in foil, flipping halfway through; panfry in a small amount of oil over medium-high heat for 3 to 4 minutes per side; or Air-Fry at 375°F (190°C) for 12 to 16 minutes.

You Are SO Vegan!

Take this one to the next level by adding veggie Bacon Strips (page 202) on toasted sourdough smeared with Aioli Dipping Sauce (page 195), served open faced smothered in maple syrup.

SWEET CARAMELIZED ONION BURGER

Gluten-Free

Sometimes sweet and savory with a bit of salty is all I crave. This burger fits the bill perfectly, especially for breakfast. For a heartier breakfast, serve this burger with some fresh asparagus spears and garlic smashed or home fried potatoes on the side.

2 tablespoons (30 ml) vegetable oil, plus more for frying (optional)

1 large white onion, julienned

5 ounces (140 g) mushrooms, chopped or sliced

2 tablespoons (30 g) minced garlic

Sea salt and pepper

2 tablespoons (30 ml) pure maple syrup

2 tablespoons (30 ml) balsamic vinegar

1 cup (160 g) rice flour

2 tablespoons (16 g) cornstarch

¼ cup (30 g) pine nuts

1 tablespoon (2 g) dried parsley

¼ teaspoon liquid smoke (optional)

YIELD: 4 BURGERS

Preheat the 2 tablespoons (30 ml) oil in a skillet over medium-high heat. Add the onion, mushrooms, and garlic. Add a pinch of sea salt to really get those onions sweating. Sauté, turning often, until the mushrooms have reduced in size by about half, or about 5 minutes.

Add the maple syrup and vinegar, lower the heat to medium, and cook for about 10 minutes longer, stirring occasionally, or until most of the liquid has been absorbed. Add a liberal amount of freshly cracked pepper to taste. Remove from the heat and let cool.

Transfer to a mixing bowl. Add the flour, cornstarch, pine nuts, parsley, and liquid smoke, and knead until a nice dough forms. If you think the mixture feels too dry, don't worry; keep kneading and it will come together, I promise.

Form into 4 patties.

Cook as desired. Bake at 350°F (180°C, or gas mark 4) for 30 minutes on a baking sheet lined with parchment or a silicone baking mat, covered loosely in foil, flipping halfway through. Panfry in a small amount of oil over medium-high heat for about 3 minutes per side, or until a nice crispy crust forms. Or, Air-Fry at 375°F (190°C) for 14 to 16 minutes.

You Are SO Vegan!

Top with sautéed mushrooms and onions over a bed of sautéed bitter greens such as collard, mustard, arugula, or kale.

O'BRIEN BURGER

Gluten-Free

No-Sugar Added

Potatoes O'Brien are an Irish breakfast treat. Bright, colorful, and crunchy peppers give this patty a great texture. Enjoy this twist on a classic for breakfast, lunch, or dinner! Serve on a toasted bun with a schmear of vegan mayo, crisp lettuce, a nice slice of juicy tomato, and some ripe avocado.

3 cups (330 g) shredded russet potatoes, rinsed in cool water and drained to prevent discoloring

1 yellow onion, diced

1 green bell pepper, cored, seeded, and diced

1 cup (240 g) nondairy sour cream, store-bought or homemade (page 198)

¼ cup (113 g) diced pimiento

Salt and pepper

3 cups (360 g) chickpea flour

Oil, for frying

YIELD: 8 BURGERS

In a large mixing bowl, combine the potatoes, onion, bell pepper, sour cream, pimiento, and salt and pepper to taste. Slowly add the chickpea flour and mix until well incorporated. The mixture should be very wet.

Form into 8 patties. Line a plate with paper towels.

Preheat ¼ inch (6 mm) oil in a large frying pan over high heat. The oil is ready when a piece of dough dropped into it sizzles immediately.

Fry each patty for 3 to 5 minutes per side, or until extra golden and crispy.

Transfer to the plate to drain the excess oil.

You Are SO Vegan!

Burrito-fy this baby by using a large flour (or gluten-free) tortilla. Start by adding some prepared black beans, then cutting the patty in half and placing on top of the beans. Top with peppery arugula and a drizzle of Chipotle Dipping Sauce (page 192.) Wrap it up and warm in a dry pan until lightly browned.

CHERRY OATMEAL PROTEIN-PACKED ENERGY BURGER

Soy-Free

These are ultra portable and keep me satisfied all the way 'til lunchtime. And, yes, they may look like cookies. But cookies for breakfast doesn't sound nearly as healthy as "Protein Packed Energy Burger" now does it?

½ cup (80 g) rice flour

½ cup (56 g) coconut flour

1 cup (80 g) quick-cooking oats

1 cup (120 g) dried cherries or your favorite dried fruit

½ cup (92 g) pea protein powder

½ cup (110 g) firmly packed brown sugar

½ cup (65 g) raw cashews or your nut of choice

¼ cup (29 g) wheat germ

¼ cup (32 g) hulled pumpkin seeds

¼ cup (32 g) hulled sunflower seeds

½ teaspoon baking powder

½ teaspoon baking soda

½ teaspoon sea salt

½ teaspoon ground cinnamon

1 container (6 ounces, or 170 g) vanilla-flavored nondairy yogurt

½ cup (120 ml) nondairy milk

¼ cup (64 g) cashew nut butter

¼ cup (84 g) agave nectar

¼ cup (60 ml melted or 56 g solid) coconut oil

—————

YIELD: 8 BURGERS

Preheat the oven to 350°F (180°C, or gas mark 4). Line a baking sheet with parchment or a silicone baking mat.

In a large mixing bowl, combine the flours, oats, dried cherries, protein powder, brown sugar, cashews, wheat germ, pumpkin seeds, sunflower seeds, baking powder, baking soda, salt, and cinnamon.

In a separate bowl, whisk together the yogurt, milk, nut butter, agave, and coconut oil.

Add the dry ingredients to the wet and mix well, using your hands, until a nice dough forms.

Divide into 8 portions. Form into patties. Place on the prepared baking sheet.

Bake, uncovered, for 18 to 20 minutes, or until the tops just start to crack.

You Are SO Vegan!

Instead of a glass of milk to wash down this cookie (I mean burger!) blend up a smoothie! Add frozen pineapple, mango, spinach, a scoop of your favorite protein powder and blend together with coconut milk. Creamy and delicious.

Chapter 3

TRADITIONAL BEEF-Y BURGERS

*Burgers that look, and taste,
like the "real" thing.*

———— • ————

SUNDAY AFTERNOON GRILLERS

Just like their animal based look-alikes, these burgers stand up to the best of them on a grill! Use these patties anywhere you want a meat-y burger patty. I love these in the Cowgirl Bacon Cheeseburger (page 160) and the Now That's a Whopper! (page 167).

2 tablespoons (30 ml) vegetable oil

1 cup (96 g) TVP (Textured Vegetable Protein) granules

1 cup (235 ml) boiling vegetable broth or water

8 ounces (227 g) mushrooms, roughly chopped

1 white onion, roughly chopped

2 cloves garlic, roughly chopped

1 cup (144 g) vital wheat gluten flour

¼ cup (30 g) nutritional yeast

¼ cup (60 ml) tamari or soy sauce

6 ounces (170 g) tomato paste

1 cup (96 g) diced scallion

YIELD: 6 TO 8 PATTIES

Preheat the oil in a flat-bottomed skillet over medium-high heat.

In a heat-safe bowl, pour boiling broth over the TVP granules, cover, and let sit for 10 minutes.

While the TVP is reconstituting, add the mushrooms, onion, and garlic to the pan. Sauté for 5 to 6 minutes, or until fragrant and beginning to brown.

In a food processor, combine the sautéed mushroom mixture, reconstituted TVP, gluten flour, nutritional yeast, tamari, and tomato paste. Process until well combined and "meaty" looking.

Transfer to a bowl and mix in the scallion. Form into 6 to 8 patties.

You can bake or fry these, but my favorite way to serve them is grilled. Use a lower flame, oil the grill, and slow cook them for about 10 minutes per side. BE PATIENT! Don't flip them too early or they will stick, and you won't get those sought-after grill marks.

These also freeze well, so you can make them in advance and bring them to your next outdoor get-together.

You Are SO Vegan!

Replace the reconstituted TVP with 1¼ cups (232 g) prepared quinoa. When preparing your quinoa, use vegetable broth instead of water for extra flavor.

WESTERN BACON CHEESEBURGER

These are inspired by what I remember a Carl's Jr. (Hardee's in some necks of the woods) Western Bacon Cheeseburger tasting like, but all in one patty. They are extremely hearty and thick, so they hold together very, very well. I suggest these be served with a dollop of barbecue sauce and a few onion rings, with some baked beans on the side.

1 cup (96 g) TVP granules

1 scant cup (225 ml) vegetable broth

¼ cup (25 g) imitation bacon bits, store-bought or homemade (page 201)

1 cup (144 g) vital wheat gluten flour

¼ teaspoon liquid smoke

½ cup (60 g) nutritional yeast

1 tablespoon (8 g) garlic powder

1 tablespoon (8 g) onion powder

¼ cup (64 g) peanut butter

¼ cup (60 ml) pure maple syrup

¼ cup (60 ml) vegetable oil

¼ cup (68 g) barbecue sauce, store-bought or homemade (page 190)

Salt and pepper

Oil, for frying (optional)

YIELD: 4 BURGERS

In a large microwave-safe bowl, mix together the TVP granules and the broth, cover tightly with plastic wrap, and microwave for 5 to 6 minutes. Alternatively, bring the broth to a boil, pour over the TVP granules, cover, and let sit for 10 minutes. Let cool.

Add the bacon bits, flour, liquid smoke, nutritional yeast, garlic powder, onion powder, peanut butter, maple syrup, oil, barbecue sauce, and salt and pepper to taste to the bowl. Knead together for at least 5 minutes, then let sit for a few minutes to thicken up.

Form into 4 patties. Refrigerate or freeze until ready to use.

Cook as desired. Panfry in oil for 3 to 5 minutes per side over medium-high heat, or until a nice crispy crust forms. Air-Fry at 375°F (190°C) for 16 to 18 minutes. Or bake them at 350°F (180°C, or gas mark 4) on a baking sheet lined with parchment or a silicone baking mat, uncovered, for 30 minutes, flipping halfway through. These are very sturdy and will hold up just fine on the grill.

You Are SO Vegan!

Mega "Wow!" if you dare to serve this behemoth up inside two grilled slices of Texas toast slathered thick with Aioli Dipping Sauce (page 195) with a nice crisp leaf of Romaine lettuce.

ALL-AMERICAN BURGER

Nut Free

No-Sugar Added

Here's a plain old burger that stands up to the grill with the best of its meaty cousins. Garnish as you would any burger. I just eat mine plain with a smidge of vegan mayo (page 197) on the bun. Add a slice of vegan cheese for an All-American Cheeseburger.

2 tablespoons (30 ml) olive oil, plus more for frying (optional)

8 ounces (227 g) mushrooms, sliced or chopped

3 cloves garlic, minced

¾ cup (180 ml) vegetable broth

1 cup (96 g) TVP granules

¼ cup (30 g) nutritional yeast

½ cup (72 g) vital wheat gluten flour

1 tablespoon (8 g) ground mustard

1 tablespoon (8 g) onion powder

¼ teaspoon liquid smoke (optional)

Salt and pepper

———————

YIELD: 4 BURGERS

In a heavy-bottom skillet, heat the oil and sauté the mushrooms and garlic for 5 to 7 minutes, or until fragrant and beginning to brown.

Add the vegetable broth and bring to a simmer.

Add the TVP granules, mix well, cover, and remove from the heat. Let sit for 10 minutes.

When cool enough to handle, add the nutritional yeast, flour, ground mustard, onion powder, liquid smoke, and salt and pepper to taste and mix well using your hands.

Place in the fridge to cool for about 20 minutes. This will help the dough stiffen up a bit.

Form into 4 patties and cook as desired.

I love to grill these on the barbecue. I use no foil and it stands up just fine. I cook them on a pretty hot spot on the grill for about 4 to 5 minutes on each side. I do rub a little extra oil on the patty before grilling to help prevent sticking.

They can also be fried in a skillet with a little oil for the same amount of time, or Air-Fried at 375°F (190°C) for 13 to 15 minutes.

You Are SO Vegan!

No recipe note here, but I am going to give you a little idea to spread some vegan love next summer. Host a neighborhood BBQ and invite all of your neighbors over. No need to tell them in advance that all the food will be vegan. Just invite them over. Make these burgers, served up with all the traditional burger fixin's, and have some potato salad (no raisins!), macaroni salad, coleslaw, and corn on the cob. This is the type of outreach that reaches people! So many fear going vegan because they fear they won't be able to eat the foods they love. They fear the loss and experience of BBQs, cookouts, and other food related events. By showing them vegan food can be familiar in flavor and just as tasty (if not tastier!) you might just win over some folks!

REALLY MEATY BURGER

Nut Free

No-Sugar Added

If there were an Atkins diet for vegans, this burger would definitely be on the menu! It is the meatiest veggie burger I've ever had. It's a bit labor-intensive, unless you make the seitan ahead of time, but OH MY! they are really meaty. This one really is a standard meaty burger that goes great with the standard fixin's (ketchup, mustard, lettuce, tomato, vegan mayo [page 197] . . .) and a side of fries.

1 cup (96 g) TVP granules

¼ cup (60 ml) soy sauce

¾ cup (180 ml) plus ⅓ cup (80 ml) vegetable broth or water, divided

2 tablespoons (30 ml) mild-flavored vegetable oil

2 cups (200 g) prepared seitan, store-bought or homemade (page 203), chopped into tiny bits

½ cup (72 g) vital wheat gluten flour

¼ cup (30 g) nutritional yeast

1 tablespoon (8 g) garlic powder

1 tablespoon (8 g) onion powder

Pepper

Oil, for frying (optional)

YIELD: 6 TO 8 BURGERS

In a microwave-safe bowl, mix together the TVP granules, soy sauce, and the ¾ cup (180 ml) broth. Cover tightly with plastic wrap, and microwave for 5 to 6 minutes. Alternatively, bring the soy sauce and broth to a boil, pour over the TVP granules, cover, and let sit for 10 minutes. Place in a large mixing bowl.

Preheat the oil in a frying pan over medium-high heat. Add the seitan and sauté until browned, but not too crispy, about 5 to 7 minutes.

Add the seitan, flour, nutritional yeast, garlic powder, onion powder, and pepper to taste to the TVP mixture. Mix well, using your hands to make sure the flour and spices get fully incorporated. Add the remaining ⅓ cup (80 ml) broth until you get a patty-able consistency.

Form into 6 to 8 patties and cook as desired.

I really like these fried for about 4 to 5 minutes per side until crispy and golden brown. Alternatively, use your Air-Fryer at 375°F (190°C) for 16 to 18 minutes. If baking, cover with a foil tent to keep moist and bake for 15 minutes per side at 350°F (180°C, or gas mark 4), until firm and warmed all the way through.

You Are SO Vegan!

Cutting carbs? Serve it up "protein style" a.k.a. bunless and wrapped in lettuce instead.

BURGER OSCAR

Veal (eew!) Oscar is a classic Swedish dish named after King Oscar II, who was partial to topping his meat (eew!) with crab (eew!), asparagus, and béarnaise sauce. Of course we've veganized it here—to make it even better—but it's still just as fancy pants, so make sure to set your table with nice white linens and get out your fanciest silver. Serve with a nice plump baked potato, smothered in nondairy butter, Nondairy Sour Cream (page 198), and chives.

FOR HOLLANDAISE THE WAY IT SHOULD TASTE SAUCE:

¼ cup (56 g) nondairy butter

2 tablespoons (16 g) all-purpose flour

1 cup (235 ml) plain soy creamer

1 tablespoon (15 ml) lemon juice

1 tablespoon (8 g) nutritional yeast

⅛ teaspoon cayenne pepper

Salt

FOR ASPARAGUS:

1 bunch asparagus

½ cup (120 ml) olive oil

¼ cup (60 ml) balsamic vinegar

Salt and pepper

FOR BURGERS:

1 recipe Steak Burger (page 50)

4 or 8 slices French or Italian bread, lightly toasted

YIELD: 4 BURGERS

To make the sauce: In a pot, melt the butter over high heat. Add the flour and whisk vigorously until smooth. Add the creamer, bring to a boil, and immediately remove from the heat. Stir in the lemon juice, nutritional yeast, cayenne, and salt to taste.

To make the asparagus: Snap each asparagus stalk at the natural break and discard the tough bottoms.

Add the asparagus, olive oil, vinegar, and salt and pepper to taste to a resealable bag or shallow dish with a tight fitting lid and shake. Let sit for about 1 hour.

In a grill pan or on a barbecue, grill the asparagus until tender, 5 to 7 minutes, turning occasionally.

Place 1 burger on 1 slice of bread. Top with one-fourth of the asparagus and then pour on the sauce. Serve open-faced or top with another slice of bread. Repeat for the remaining 3 burgers.

Serve any remaining sauce in small bowls for dipping.

You Are SO Vegan!

Add the crab (eew!) component by soaking steamed carrot ribbons made with a vegetable peeler (5 bonus vegan points if you use a mixture of white and orange carrots for effect!) in hijiki broth for at least an hour. Make the hijiki broth by soaking a small handful of hijiki seaweed in warm water. Once marinated, strain and use as "imitation crab" on top of the burger.

BLT AND AVOCADO BURGER

Nut Free

Let me start off by saying that there is a ridiculous amount of imitation bacon bits in this recipe. Seriously, though, what's a BLT without a ton of bacon? Serve on a toasted sourdough bun with a schmear of vegan mayo (page 197) and, of course, a thick tomato slice and a nice leaf of crispy lettuce. Feel free to throw some bacon bits on top for good measure!

1 cup (144 g) vital wheat gluten flour

1 cup (125 g) all-purpose flour

1 cup (80 g) imitation bacon bits, store-bought or homemade (page 201)

1 tablespoon (8 g) garlic powder

1 tablespoon (8 g) onion powder

½ teaspoon ground black pepper

1 cup (180 g) diced tomatoes

¼ cup (60 ml) vegetable oil

2 tablespoons (30 ml) steak sauce

2 tablespoons (30 g) ketchup

2 ripe avocados

YIELD: 4 HUGE BURGERS

In a large bowl, combine the flours, bacon bits, garlic powder, onion powder, and pepper. In a separate bowl, mix together the tomatoes, oil, steak sauce, and ketchup. Add the wet ingredients to the dry and knead together until uniformly mixed. Let sit for 20 minutes.

Preheat the oven to 350°F (180°C, or gas mark 4). Line a baking sheet with parchment or a silicone baking mat.

Divide the mixture into 8 equal pieces, and flatten each piece Place ½ avocado, mushed, into the center of 4 of the flattened pieces. Sandwich with the remaining 4 pieces and pinch the edges to seal.

Bake, covered in foil, for 20 minutes, then flip and bake for 15 minutes longer, or until firm.

You Are SO Vegan!

Make baked avocado fries to up the avocado goodness. Carefully slice a firm but ripe avocado into wedges. Coat with panko bread crumbs seasoned with salt, pepper, dried parsley, and garlic powder to taste. Bake at 425°F (220°C, or gas mark 7) for 5 to 7 minutes, or until breadcrumbs begin to brown. Serve with Chipotle Dipping Sauce (page 192).

BRISBANE BURGER FROM DOWN UNDER

Vegemite. Need I say more? Oh, and don't forget to grill these babies up on the bar-bee. Serve this burger on toast with a thin layer of Vegemite spread evenly to add that salty, savory, tangy flavor the Aussies have come to know and love.

2 cups (288 g) vital wheat gluten flour

½ cup (60 g) whole wheat flour

½ cup (64 g) vegetable broth powder

1 tablespoon (6 g) freshly ground black pepper

1 cup (235 ml) water

¼ cup (68 g) ketchup

¼ cup (60 ml) vegetable oil

2 tablespoons (30 ml) soy sauce

1 tablespoon (15 ml) steak sauce

2 teaspoons (13 g) Vegemite

YIELD: 8 BURGERS

In a mixing bowl, combine the flours, vegetable broth powder, and pepper.

In a separate bowl, whisk together the water, ketchup, oil, soy sauce, steak sauce, and Vegemite.

Add the wet ingredients to the dry and knead together until well incorporated. Cover and let sit for about 20 minutes to rest.

Form into 8 patties.

Barbecue over medium heat, 5 to 7 minutes per side. Or, bake at 350°F (180°C, or gas mark 4) on a baking sheet lined with parchment or a silicone baking mat, covered loosely with foil, for 15 minutes, and then flip and bake for 15 minutes longer, until firm and warmed all the way through.

You Are SO Vegan!

Can't find Vegemite? Try the British version, Marmite, but don't tell the Aussies that I told you to!

WHISKEY BURGER

Nut Free

This one is inspired by all of the bar and pub food that has been so popular of late. The problem is, while most of it looks delicious, it is almost always riddled with hipster-sounding (nonvegan) ingredients, such as rendered pork fat. Yuck! This is a great burger to serve to friends who are over for a casual dinner or game night. It's high on flavor and richness and low on unnecessary body parts.

FOR THE WHISKEY GLAZE:

¾ cup (180 ml) orange juice

½ cup (120 ml) water

½ cup (120 ml) whiskey

¼ cup (60 ml) soy sauce or tamari

½ cup (110 g) brown sugar

2 tablespoons (20 g) minced garlic

1 tablespoon (15 g) Dijon mustard

1 teaspoon powdered ginger

½ teaspoon red chili flakes

1 tablespoon (8 g) cornstarch mixed with 2 tablespoons (30 ml) water to make a slurry

FOR THE BURGERS:

Oil, for frying

1 recipe All-American Burgers (page 38), prepared up until cooking instructions

8 slices cracked wheat sourdough bread

½ cup (120 ml) vegan mayo, store-bought or homemade (page 197)

½ cup (120 ml) Aioli Dipping Sauce (page 195)

½ cup (28 g) Crispy Fried Onions (page 222)

YIELD: 4 BURGERS AND 2 CUPS (470 ML) GLAZE

To make the whiskey glaze: Bring orange juice, water, whiskey, and soy sauce to a boil. Reduce to a simmer, add in brown sugar, and stir to dissolve. Stir in garlic, mustard, ginger, and chili flakes. Continue to simmer for 10 more minutes.

Slowly whisk in the slurry and continue to whisk until glaze thickens. Remove from heat.

To make the burgers: Preheat a frying pan or skillet with a smidge of oil over medium heat. Add patties to the pan and fry until browned, three to four minutes. Spoon glaze over the patties as they cook. Flip and repeat on the other side.

While burgers are cooking, prepare the bread by spreading each side of each piece with mayo. In a separate pan, fry the bread over medium-high heat until golden and toasty, the way a grilled cheese looks!

Remove bread from pan and spread with Aioli. Add a glazed burger to one piece of bread, top with Crispy Fried Onions, and drizzle with additional glaze. Top with another piece of toasted sourdough. Repeat with remaining burgers.

You Are SO Vegan!

In addition to the Crispy Fried Onions, top with sautéed mushrooms and caramelized onions before drizzling on the extra glaze. For a nice added tang, swap out the Aioli Dipping Sauce for Sun Dried Tomato Aioli (page 193).

MEATLOAF BURGER

Nut Free

Growing up, the best thing about meatloaf for dinner was meatloaf sandwiches for lunch the next day! These burgers make "leftovers" without having to make dinner first! I like these on a toasted white roll with the usual burger fixin's: a schmear of vegan mayo (page 197), a thick slice of onion, a pickle, some greens, a tomato slice, and a nice big dollop of ketchup. If serving for dinner, mashed potatoes are the perfect side.

3 cups (288 g) TVP granules

2½ cups (590 ml) vegetable broth or water

2 tablespoons (30 ml) soy sauce or tamari

2 tablespoons (30 ml) olive oil

1 large yellow onion, finely diced

2 cloves garlic, minced

1 teaspoon ground black pepper

1 tablespoon (8 g) garlic powder

1 tablespoon (8 g) onion powder

½ teaspoon cumin

1 cup (240 g) ketchup or barbecue sauce, store-bought or homemade (page 190), plus extra for basting

1½ cups (216 g) vital wheat gluten flour

YIELD: 8 BURGERS

Preheat the oven to 350°F (180°C, or gas mark 4). Line a baking sheet with parchment or a silicone baking mat.

In a microwave-safe bowl, mix together the TVP granules, broth, and soy sauce, cover tightly with plastic wrap, and microwave for 5 to 6 minutes. Alternatively, bring the broth and soy sauce to a boil, pour over the TVP granules, cover, and let stand for 10 minutes. Set aside to cool.

In a skillet, heat the olive oil and sauté the onion and garlic until translucent and just beginning to brown, 7 to 10 minutes.

Add to the reconstituted TVP, along with the pepper, garlic powder, onion powder, cumin, 1 cup (240 g) ketchup, and flour. Mix well. Use your hands and knead the mixture together. Make sure everything is well incorporated. Let the mixture sit for at least 20 minutes, to let the gluten develop.

Form into 8 patties and place on the prepared baking sheet.

Bake, uncovered, for 15 minutes.

Remove from the oven and brush with the additional ketchup, return to the oven, and bake for 15 minutes longer, or until firm and the ketchup begins to turn a dark caramelized crimson.

You Are SO Vegan!

Instead of making these as burgers, make them into Shepherds Pie! Press the burger mixture into 8 ramekins and top with a mixture of sautéed onions, mushrooms, and peas. Pipe the top with mashed potatoes and bake until nice and hot and the tips of the potatoes are browned.

NOOCHY BURGER

No-Sugar Added

This burger was made for the love of the nooch! I like to keep the fixin's simple on this one because the taste of this patty is pretty rich: a little vegan mayo (page 197), maybe some avocado and some ketchup, if you must, on a soft white sesame seed bun.

1 cup (96 g) TVP granules

1 cup (235 ml) vegetable broth

½ cup (128 g) cashew nut butter

¼ cup (64 g) tahini paste

½ cup (120 g) nondairy sour cream, store-bought or homemade (page 198)

2 tablespoons (36 g) white or yellow miso

½ cup (60 g) nutritional yeast

1 cup (144 g) vital wheat gluten flour

1 tablespoon (8 g) garlic powder

1 tablespoon (8 g) onion powder

1 tablespoon (7 g) paprika

¼ teaspoon turmeric

1 teaspoon dried parsley or 1 tablespoon (4 g) chopped fresh parsley

Salt and pepper

Oil, for frying (optional)

YIELD: 6 BURGERS

In a microwave-safe bowl, mix together the TVP granules and broth, cover tightly with plastic wrap, and microwave for 5 to 6 minutes. Alternatively, bring the broth to a boil, pour over the TVP granules and cover. Let sit for 10 minutes until cool.

In a mixing bowl, combine the nut butter, tahini, sour cream, and miso. Add the reconstituted TVP and mix well.

In a separate bowl, combine the nutritional yeast, flour, garlic powder, onion powder, paprika, turmeric, parsley, and salt and pepper to taste.

Add the dry ingredients to the wet and knead together until a nice dough forms.

Form into 6 patties and cook as desired.

Fry in oil until golden and crispy, 3 to 5 minutes per side; Air-Fry at 375°F (190°C) for 16 to 18 minutes, or bake in the oven at 350°F (180°C, or gas mark 4), on a baking sheet lined with parchment or a silicone baking mat, loosely covered in foil, for 15 minutes, and then flip and bake for 15 minutes longer, until firm and warmed all the way through.

You Are SO Vegan!

Prove your love for the nooch by serving these drowning in noochy Cheesy Sauce (see Zucchini Mushroom Burger page 110) with a side of noochy mac and cheese (see Mac and Cheese Burger page 172)!

ALOHA TERIYAKI BURGER

Nut Free

Take your tummy on a tropical vacation. My favorite getaway is Maui, and whenever I make these, I pretend I am sitting on the sandy white beach at Ka'anapali watching the locals dive off Black Rock. These are delicious on a grilled bun with lettuce, grilled Maui onions, and a thick, grilled pineapple ring.

1 cup (96 g) TVP granules

¾ cup (180 ml) vegetable broth or water

2 tablespoons (30 ml) soy sauce

2 tablespoons (30 ml) teriyaki sauce, plus extra for frying

2½ tablespoons (19 g) ground flax-seed mixed with 3 tablespoons (45 ml) water

1 cup (155 g) crushed pineapple

2 tablespoons (28 g) brown sugar

½ cup (72 g) vital wheat gluten flour

½ cup (60 g) whole wheat flour

Salt and pepper

YIELD: 6 BURGERS

In a microwave-safe bowl, combine the TVP granules, vegetable broth, soy sauce, and 2 tablespoons (30 ml) teriyaki. Cover tightly with plastic wrap and microwave for 5 to 6 minutes. Alternatively, bring the vegetable stock, soy sauce, and teriyaki to a boil in a pot, add to the TVP in a bowl, cover, and let stand for 10 minutes. Let cool.

Add the flax egg (the flaxseed and water mixture), pineapple, brown sugar, and flours. Season with salt and pepper to taste.

Mix well with your hands for about 5 minutes. The mixture should end up being a little sticky and stringy. Depending on the moisture level of your TVP and pineapple, you may need to add more or less flour. Refrigerate for at least 20 minutes to thicken up a bit. Form into 6 patties.

In a nonstick pan or skillet, panfry the patties, adding more teriyaki sauce to taste. The teriyaki will caramelize and make a nice dark crust.

You Are SO Vegan!

Make your own quick and easy teriyaki sauce from scratch! Mix together 1 cup (235 ml) water, ¼ cup (60 ml) soy sauce, ¼ cup (55 g) brown sugar, ½ teaspoon powdered ginger, and 1 teaspoon minced garlic in a saucepan over medium heat. Bring to a simmer. Slowly stir in a slurry made of 2 tablespoons (16 g) cornstarch mixed with ¼ cup (60 ml) cold water. Continue to cook, stirring constantly until sauce is thick and shiny.

STEAK BURGER

Nut Free

This beefy burger is reminiscent of a steak house filet mignon. The glaze is silky, and savory, and luscious, and gives the final patties an extra bit of that something you can't quite put your finger on, but you know you've tasted it before . . . umami. The glaze makes more than you will need for the burgers, so make sure to use it on other things, like stir-fry, rice bowls, and to toss with your favorite veggie proteins.

FOR THE SEITAN DOUGH:

1 can (20 ounce, [565 g]) young green jackfruit, in brine, rinsed, drained and patted dry

1 ½ cups (216 g) vital wheat gluten

¼ cup (31 g) all-purpose flour

1 tablespoon (8 g) dried minced onion

1 teaspoon garlic powder

1 teaspoon dried parsley

¼ teaspoon salt

¼ teaspoon black pepper

1 cup (235 ml) beef-flavored vegetable broth

¼ cup (60 ml) vegan Worcestershire sauce

2 tablespoons (30 ml) mild-flavored vegetable oil

FOR THE SIMMERING BROTH:

6 cups (1.4 L) water

½ cup (120 ml) soy sauce

¼ cup (60 ml) vegan Worcestershire sauce

2 tablespoons (20 g) minced garlic

2 tablespoons (16g) onion powder

½ teaspoon black pepper

To make the seitan dough: Preheat oven to 375°F (190°C, or gas mark 5) and line a baking sheet with parchment or a reusable baking mat. Arrange jackfruit chunks in a single layer and bake uncovered for 30 minutes.

While jackfruit is baking, mix together vital wheat gluten, all-purpose flour, onion, garlic powder, parsley, salt, and pepper to a medium-size mixing bowl.

In a separate bowl combine broth, Worcesterchire, and oil.

Remove jackfruit from oven and allow it to cool, enough to handle. Shred the jackfruit until it resembles shredded chicken (you can use your fingertips to do this) and add to the dry mixture. Toss to coat.

Add wet mixture to dry and, using your hands, mix until fully combined. Right in the bowl, knead the mixture for 15 full minutes, ripping it apart into small chunks and smashing it back together as you go. (You can also use a stand mixer with a dough hook, or a food processor with a dough blade for this.) Bits and pieces of the jackfruit will fall out of the dough, that's okay, just smash it back in. The simmering process will lock it into place. Form into a ball, cover lightly, and allow to rest for twenty minutes.

To make the simmering broth: Add all ingredients to a medium pot, with a lid, and stir to combine.

Lay a sheet of cheesecloth, about 12 inches (30 cm) square, on a flat surface. Place rested dough ball in the center of the cheesecloth. Roll tightly into a log shape, about 4 inches (10 cm) in diameter, and 4 inches (10 cm) long, and tie the ends closed. Place in simmering broth.

FOR THE SAVORY STEAK GLAZE:

2 cups reserved simmering broth

¼ cup (55 g) tightly packed brown sugar

¼ cup (60 ml) water

2 tablespoons (16 g) cornstarch

YOU WILL ALSO NEED:

Cheesecloth

Oil, for frying

—————

YIELD: 4 TO 6 BURGERS

Cover and bring to a simmer. Simmer for 2 hours, returning occasionally to rotate and prevent it from sticking to the bottom of the pot, especially if it is not fully submerged in broth.

Remove from broth (do not discard broth!) and allow to cool completely. You can even place in the refrigerator in an airtight container, for up to a week, before using.

To make the savory steak glaze: Bring 2 cups (475 ml) reserved simmering broth to a boil, reduce to a simmer. Add in brown sugar and stir to dissolve. Mix together water and cornstarch to make a slurry. Slowly whisk in the slurry and continue to whisk until glaze thickens. Remove from heat.

Once seitan has cooled, unwrap the cheesecloth. Using a sharp serrated knife, slice the log into burger patties to desired thickness. (I usually do ¾-inch [2-cm] thick slices to really make them like a steak. Depending on how you are going to serve them, you may want a thinner cut.)

Preheat a frying pan or skillet with a smidge of oil over medium heat. Add patties to the pan and fry until browned, 3 to 4 minutes. Spoon glaze over the patties as they cook. Flip and repeat on the other side.

Serve as desired.

You Are SO Vegan!

Instead of serving this as a burger, serve it as a steak! Serve on a bed of creamy mashed potatoes with grilled asparagus and sautéed mushrooms on top with lots of extra glaze drizzled over the whole shebang.

Chapter 4

BEAN-BASED BURGERS

Full of protein, fiber, flavor, and fun!

SESAME BEAN BÁNH MÌ BURGER

This non traditional twist on the bánh mì is as beautiful as it is delicious.

FOR THE QUICK PICKLED VEGETABLES:

½ cup (54 g) shredded carrots

½ cup (8 g) chopped cilantro

½ cup (50 g) chopped green onion

10 radishes, thinly sliced

3 stalks celery, chopped

1 cucumber, half moon slices

3 cups (705 ml) water

⅓ cup (80 ml) white vinegar

2 tablespoons (36 g) salt

FOR THE BURGERS:

2 cups (240 g) walnut pieces

1 can (15 ounces [425 g]) chickpeas, with the liquid

1 cup (30 g) packed baby spinach leaves (a generous handful)

½ cup (80 g) diced yellow onion

2 tablespoons (30 ml) sesame oil

½ teaspoon salt

¼ cup (30 g) nutritional yeast

¼ cup (26 g) ground flaxseed

¼ cup (24 g) almond flour

¼ cup (30 g) oat flour

½ cup (72 g) sesame seeds (black, white, or a mix of both)

¼ cup (4g) chopped cilantro, optional, as garnish

YIELD: 6 BURGERS

To make the quick pickled vegetables: Add all the vegetables, water, vinegar, and salt to gallon-size resealable plastic bag. Shake to combine and remove as much of the air out of the bag as possible. Store in the refrigerator until ready to use.

Preheat oven to 350°F (180°C, or gas mark 4). Have ready a baking sheet lined with parchment or a reusable baking mat.

To make the burgers: Add walnut pieces, chickpeas with liquid, spinach, onion, oil, and salt to a food processor and purée until well combined but still a little chunky. Transfer to a bowl and stir in nutritional yeast, flaxseed, almond flour, and oat flour. Your mixture should be thick, but not dry, and able to hold a burger shape when formed. If your mixture is too wet, add in a little more flour. If too dry, add a little water, 1 teaspoon at a time. Place the sesame seeds in a shallow dish. Form mixture into 6 patties and place in the seeds to coat.

Bake for 20 minutes, flip and bake an additional 20 minutes. Cool for a few minutes to firm up. Serve on a bun, topped with the quick pickled vegetables, cilantro, and a liberal drizzle of Creamy Sesame Sriracha Sauce (page 200).

You Are SO Vegan!

For a more authentic bánh mì experience, serve this on a baguette. Spread smashed avocado on both sides of the bread, and add fresh sliced jalapeños to the pickled vegetables. Serve with a spicy chili sauce made by mixing together equal parts sriracha and agave and thinning it out a little with a bit of rice vinegar.

CINCO DE MAYO BURGER

Nut Free

No-Sugar Added

Feliz Cinco de Mayo! Serve with tortilla chips and salsa or guacamole, or with Spanish rice and beans. To garnish, think burrito fillings: avocado, nondairy sour cream, salsa, peppers, onions . . . .

12 ounces (340 g) soy chorizo

1 can (15 ounces [425 g]) *frijoles negro* (black beans), drained

1 cup (125 g) all-purpose flour

½ cup (50 g) chopped scallion

½ cup (8 g) finely chopped fresh cilantro

Oil or nonstick spray, for frying

YIELD: 5 BURGERS (OF COURSE!)

In a skillet, panfry soy chorizo and beans until they are completely warmed through and hot, 5 to 7 minutes.

Remove from the heat and stir in the flour. Let cool.

Using your hands, knead in the scallion and cilantro until you get a soft, smooth mixture.

Form into 5 patties and panfry in a smidge of oil over medium heat until a nice crispy crust forms, about 3 to 5 minutes per side.

You Are SO Vegan!

Looking for a drink to serve at your fiesta? Don't rely on artificially flavored, artificially colored, sickeningly sweet premade margarita mixes. Making a real margarita is simple: Add 4 ounces (118 ml) tequila, 3 ounces (89 ml) fresh lime juice, 1 ounce (20 ml) simple syrup, and 3 ounces (89 ml) triple sec to a shaker filled with ice cubes. Shake and pour into a salt-rimmed glass with a wedge of lime.

BASIC BLACK BEAN BBQ BURGER

This hearty, meaty burger is a great burger to serve up to meat lovers. I know whenever I do, they love 'em and the cow burgers get left behind as these get gobbled up. These taste great at a barbecue on a Soft White Bun (page 206) with a dollop of guacamole. Serve with some potato and corn on the cob.

1 cup (96 g) TVP granules

1 scant cup (225 ml) water

½ cup (80 g) diced onion

1 can (15 ounces [425 g]) black beans, drained and rinsed

¾ cup (204 g) barbecue sauce, store-bought or homemade (page 190)

1 tablespoon (8 g) onion powder

1 tablespoon (8 g) garlic powder

1 teaspoon black pepper

3 tablespoons (48 g) peanut butter

½ cup (56 g) soy flour

Oil, for frying (optional)

YIELD: 8 BURGERS

In a microwave-safe bowl, mix together the TVP granules and the water, cover tightly with plastic wrap, and microwave for 5 to 6 minutes. Alternatively, bring the water to a boil, pour over the TVP granules, cover, and let sit for 10 minutes.

When the TVP is cool enough to handle, mix in the onion, beans, barbecue sauce, onion powder, garlic powder, pepper, peanut butter, and flour. Using your hands, knead the dough to incorporate the ingredients fully, and until the TVP granules are no longer the consistency of granules. This will be about 5 minutes of hand manipulation. If your dough is too dry, add a bit of oil to the mix.

Refrigerate for at least 20 minutes.

Form into 8 patties and cook as desired. If baking, place on a baking sheet lined with parchment or a silicone baking mat and bake for 30 minutes at 350°F (180°C, or gas mark 4), loosely covered with a foil tent, flipping halfway through. If frying in oil, cook for 3 to 4 minutes per side, until a nice crispy golden crust forms. If using your Air-Fryer, set it at 375°F (190°C) for 16 to 18 minutes. These stand up well on the grill, too!

You Are SO Vegan!

Serve topped with a tangy slaw made with grated broccoli stems, chopped cilantro, and Tangy Tahini Sauce (page 189).

LIZZY'S LENTIL BURGER

Soy-Free   Gluten-Free
No-Sugar Added   Nut Free

My besties, Lizzy and Tony, were the ones who really got me interested in international cuisine way back when we were in our twenties! They were the only ones I knew who had traveled outside the country! This one is for you Lizzy! Influenced by Indian flavors found in Daal, this lentil burger is great served bunless topped with Tangy Tahini Sauce (page 189).

¼ cup (48 g) dried red lentils*

¼ cup (48 g) dried green lentils

¼ cup (56 g) dried split peas

1 pound (454 g) red potatoes, skin on, cut into chunks

2 tablespoons (30 ml) sesame oil

1 yellow onion, diced

4 cloves garlic, minced

1 teaspoon cumin

1 teaspoon coriander

1 teaspoon garam masala

¼ teaspoon turmeric

¼ to ½ cup (30 to 60 g) chickpea flour

Oil, for frying (optional)

*If you can't get red lentils, it's okay—just use all green.

YIELD: 8 BURGERS

Fill a large pot with salted water and add the lentils and split peas. Bring to a boil. Boil for 15 minutes, then add the potatoes. Boil for 15 minutes longer, or until the potatoes are fork-tender.

Meanwhile, heat the oil in a skillet and sauté the onion and garlic until translucent, 5 to 7 minutes. Add the cumin, coriander, garam masala, and turmeric, stir to combine, and sauté for 2 or 3 more minutes.

After the lentils and potatoes are done, strain and return them to the pot. Add the onion and garlic mixture. With a hand potato masher, mash all the ingredients together. Let sit or refrigerate until cool, at least 20 minutes, or even overnight.

Preheat the oven to 350°F (180°C, or gas mark 4). Line a baking sheet with parchment or a silicone mat, or spray with cooking spray.

Add the flour to the mixture, starting with ¼ cup (30 g) and adding more if needed. Knead until the flour is well incorporated. Form into 8 patties and place on the prepared baking sheet. Bake for 15 minutes per side, covered in a foil tent, until firm and warmed all the way through. These can also be Air-Fried, at 395°F (201°C) for 14 to 16 minutes.

You Are SO Vegan!

Wrap it up! On a flour tortilla, layer on a fragrant rice, *(Add 1 cup [180 g] basmati rice, 2 cups [470 ml] vegetable stock, ¼ teaspoon each of cinnamon, ground cumin, and ground cardamom to a rice cooker. Once cooked, stir in ¼ cup [31 g] chopped pistachios*, ¼ cup [30 g] currants, and 2 tablespoons [30 ml] melted vegan butter)*, a burger patty, halved, mixed greens, and Tangy Tahini Sauce (page 189). Wrap it all up nice and tight and heat in a dry pan until browned.
*Leave out the pistachios to keep it nut-free.

"TRAVIS LOVES CILANTRO" BURGER

Travis was one of the kindest, caring people I have ever known. And he was funny as all get out. Over a decade ago, when I originally wrote this book, I asked Travis what he would like in a burger. He exclaimed, "CILANTRO! CILANTRO! CILANTRO!" And he wasn't talking about garnish. He wanted lots of the green stuff throughout the burger. So, cilantro haters beware, this one just screams with it. This one's for you, Travis. #fuckcancer. (Serve it on a toasted bun topped with salsa or nondairy sour cream, avocado, and a thick juicy slice of red tomato.)

1 cup (96 g) TVP granules

3 tablespoons (24 g) taco seasoning, store-bought or homemade (page 201)

1 cup (235 ml) water or vegetable broth

¼ cup (60 ml) canola oil

1 can (15 ounces [425 g]) black or pinto beans, drained

1 bunch fresh cilantro, leaves chopped (stems discarded)

1 cup (144 g) vital wheat gluten flour

1 cup (125 g) all-purpose flour

¾ cup (180 g) nondairy sour cream, store-bought or homemade (page 198)

YIELD: 6 BURGERS

Preheat the oven to 350°F (180°C, or gas mark 4). Line a baking sheet with parchment or a silicone baking mat.

In a microwave-safe dish, combine the TVP granules and taco seasoning, and then add the water. Cover tightly with plastic wrap and microwave for 5 to 6 minutes. Alternatively, bring the water to a boil, pour over the TVP granules and taco seasoning, cover, and let sit for 10 minutes. Let cool.

Add the oil, beans, and cilantro and stir to combine. Using your hands, knead in the flours until well incorporated. Add the sour cream and knead again.

Form into 6 patties and place on the prepared baking sheet. Bake, uncovered, for 15 to 20 minutes, then flip and bake for 15 minutes longer, until firm and just beginning to brown.

You Are SO Vegan!

Serve with tortilla chips, salsa, and a side of Cilantro Lime Rice (page 227) for a fiesta in your mouth!

KOREAN BBQ BURGER

Gluten-Free   Soy-Free

Spicy with a hint of sweet, these burgers were inspired by some Korean spicy fries that I got off a food truck in Long Beach, California—so good! If soy and wheat are not issues for you, I suggest serving these on a soft white bun, lightly toasted and schmeared with nondairy cream cheese mixed with a little bit of Sriracha sauce.

---

1 tablespoon (15 ml) sesame oil

1 to 3 tablespoons (15 to 45 g) chili garlic sauce or Sambal Oelek

4 cloves garlic, minced

1 cup (57 g) instant potato flakes

1 can (15 ounces [425 g]) white beans, drained and rinsed

2 tablespoons (12 g) finely chopped scallion or chives

½ cup (65 g) raw cashews, finely ground into a powder

2 tablespoons (42 g) agave nectar

2 tablespoons (16 g) cornstarch

3 tablespoons (45 ml) canola oil

Salt and pepper

Oil, for frying (optional)

YIELD: 4 BURGERS

Add all the ingredients to a mixing bowl, and mash together using your hands. Really smoosh it together until there are almost no whole beans left in the mixture. Let rest for at least 20 minutes to thicken up a bit.

Form into 4 patties.

Panfry in oil over medium-high heat for 2 to 3 minutes per side, or until a golden, crispy crust is formed, or bake, uncovered, on a baking sheet lined with parchment or a silicone baking mat at 350°F (180°C, or gas mark 4) for 25 minutes, or until firm and just beginning to brown.

You Are SO Vegan!

Add a little crunch by serving with a light and crisp cabbage slaw. Toss shredded green or purple cabbage with a bit of rice vinegar and season with red chili flakes to taste.

CONFETTI BURGER

Gluten-Free

Soy-Free

Nut Free

No-Sugar Added

The bright colors in this patty remind me of a party, hence the name confetti. Enjoy this festive little guy on a toasted gluten-free bun schmeared with Aioli Dipping Sauce (page 195) alongside some Baked Sweet Potato Fries (page 216).

1 cup (225 g) dried split peas

1 cup (192 g) dried green or black lentils

4 cups (940 ml) vegetable broth

2 tablespoons (30 ml) olive oil

2 cups (298 g) diced red, yellow, and green bell peppers

1 cup (160 g) diced red onion

2 tablespoons (30 g) minced garlic

2 tablespoons (33 g) tomato paste

1 teaspoon curry powder

1 teaspoon chipotle powder

¼ cup (64 g) tahini

2 tablespoons (30 ml) sesame oil

½ cup (122 g) unsweetened apple-sauce

Salt and pepper

2 cups (114 g) instant potato flakes

Oil, for frying (optional)

YIELD: 10 TO 12 BURGERS

In a large stockpot, combine the peas, lentils, and broth and bring to a boil. Boil hard for 4 minutes. Reduce to a simmer, cover, and simmer until tender. Depending on the age of the beans, it could take as little as 10 minutes or as long as an hour, so keep a watchful eye. Drain.

While the peas and lentils are cooking, preheat the olive oil in a flat skillet over medium-high heat. Add the peppers and onion and sauté until tender, 5 to 7 minutes. Add the garlic, and cook for 2 to 3 minutes longer. Remove from the heat and transfer to a large mixing bowl, along with the fully cooked and drained lentils and peas. Let cool.

Add the tomato paste, curry powder, chipotle powder, tahini, sesame oil, applesauce, and salt and pepper to taste. Mash together until well incorporated.

Begin adding the potato flakes a little bit at a time, kneading until you get a nice patty-able consistency.

Form into 10 to 12 patties and cook as desired.

Bake, covered in foil, at 350°F (180°C, or gas mark 4) for 15 minutes, then flip and bake for 15 minutes longer, until firm. Or, panfry in oil for 3 to 5 minutes per side until a golden crust forms. Alternatively, use your Air-Fryer at 375°F (190°C) for 14 to 16 minutes.

You Are SO Vegan!

Bowl-ify it! Start with a base of basmati rice. Add steamed broccoli and cauliflower. Top with crumbled Confetti Burger and drizzle with Tangy Tahini Sauce (page 189).

THREE BEAN CHILI BURGER

I love a big bowl of chili. This recipe starts with a nice chili recipe, and then whammo, turns it into a burger!

FOR CHILI:

1 can (15 ounces [425 g]) pinto beans, with liquid

1 can (15 ounces [425 g]) black beans, with liquid

1 can (15 ounces [425 g]) red or kidney beans, with liquid

4 ounces (112 g) jarred jalapeño slices

6 ounces (170 g) tomato paste

1 tablespoon (6 g) black pepper

2 tablespoons (16 g) garlic powder

1 tablespoon (8 g) onion powder

1 tablespoon (8 g) chili powder

1 teaspoon ground cumin

1 cup (160 g) finely diced white or yellow onion

1 cup (235 ml) vegetable broth

Salt

1 cup (96 g) TVP granules

FOR BURGERS:

½ recipe chili (above)

2 cups (240 g) masa harina flour (I like Maseca brand)

⅓ cup (80 ml) vegetable oil, plus more for frying (optional)

—————

YIELD: ABOUT 8 CUPS (2K) CHILI, OR 8 BURGERS

To make the chili: In a large stockpot, combine all the beans, jalapeño, tomato paste, pepper, garlic powder, onion powder, chili powder, cumin, onion, broth, and salt to taste. Mix well.

Bring to a boil, lower the heat to a simmer, cover, and let simmer for at least 20 minutes. Uncover, stir in the TVP granules, remove from the heat, recover, and let sit for at least 10 minutes. Let cool. Divide the recipe in half and refrigerate one half for another use.

To make the burgers: In a large bowl, add the flour and the ⅓ cup (80 ml) oil to the reserved half of the chili. Knead together well.

Form into 8 patties. Cook as desired.

To fry, panfry in oil over medium heat for about 5 minutes per side, or until a golden crispy crust forms. Alternatively, use your Air-Fryer at 375°F (190°C) for 16 to 18 minutes. To bake, bake at 350°F (180°C, or gas mark 4) on a baking sheet lined with parchment or a silicone baking mat, lightly covered in foil to prevent drying out, for about 15 minutes per side, until firm and warmed all the way through.

You Are SO Vegan!

Serve open-faced with the remaining chili and all of your favorite chili toppers, such as Nondairy Sour Cream (page 198, and pictured here), diced onion, guacamole, scallions, and, if it tickles your fancy, some Nacho Cheesy Sauce (page 188).

FALAFEL BURGER

These may not be the ball shape you are used to, but they certainly do pop with all of the falafel flavors you know and love. Serve in a pita with Tzatziki Sauce (page 199) and some fresh, crunchy vegetables.

Soy-Free No-Sugar Added Nut Free

2 cups (480 g) fully cooked chickpeas (I use canned)

1 cup (235 ml) vegetable broth

1 cup (160 g) diced onion

2 tablespoons (24 g) potato starch dissolved in ¼ cup (60 ml) water to make a slurry

⅓ cup (80 ml) olive oil, plus more for frying

½ cup (8 g) finely chopped fresh cilantro (or parsley [30 g] for you cilantro haters!)

1 teaspoon ground coriander

½ teaspoon ground cumin

½ teaspoon cayenne pepper

2 tablespoons (30 ml) lemon juice

1 cup (120 g) whole wheat flour

1½ to 2 cups (180 to 240 g) chickpea (garbanzo) flour

Salt and pepper

YIELD: 6 BURGERS

Combine the chickpeas, vegetable broth, and onion in a large pot. Bring to a boil, lower the heat to a simmer, and simmer, uncovered, for 15 minutes.

Mix in the potato starch slurry, remove from the heat, and stir well to thicken. Transfer to a mixing bowl and mash with a fork or potato masher.

Add the ⅓ cup (80 ml) olive oil, cilantro, coriander, cumin, cayenne, lemon juice, whole wheat flour, 1½ cups (180 g) of the chickpea flour, and salt and pepper to taste. Knead until a nice elastic dough is formed, adding some of the remaining ½ cup (60 g) chickpea flour, a little bit at a time, if your dough is too sticky.

Preheat the oven to 350°F (180°C, or gas mark 4) and line a baking sheet with parchment or a silicone mat.

Form into 6 patties and place on the prepared baking sheet.

Bake for 20 minutes, uncovered.

Preheat a pan with olive oil and panfry the baked burgers for 3 to 5 minutes per side to get a nice golden crispy crust. A panini press or tabletop electric grill (like a George Foreman) also works well as an alternative to frying after you bake it.

You Are SO Vegan!

Okay, so making the sacred falafel ball into a burger patty wasn't sacrilegious enough for you? Alrighty, then. Instead of patties, shape these into log shape and serve them hot dog style in a nice toasty white bun topped with Tzatziki Sauce (page 199) and pickled veggies.

CURRIED SPLIT PEA BURGER

Other than the cooking of the peas, these tasty burgers come together quickly and easily. If you are really into curry, the way I am, feel free to double the amount listed in the recipe. Serve piping hot on a piece of 50/50 Flatbread (page 207) or pita with some Tzatziki Sauce (page 199). If you choose a nonsoy-based yogurt, this one is also soy free. Choose a nut-free yogurt and it will be nut-free.

3 cups (705 ml) lightly salted water

1 cup (225 g) dried split peas

3 tablespoons (45 ml) sesame oil

1 tablespoon (6 g) curry powder

1 container (6 ounces, or 170 g) plain unsweetened nondairy yogurt

1 cup (120 g) whole wheat flour

Salt and pepper

Olive oil, for frying (optional)

—————

YIELD: 4 TO 6 BURGERS

In a stockpot, bring the salted water and split peas to a boil, lower the heat to a simmer, and cook until the peas are tender, about 30 minutes, or until most of the moisture is absorbed. You can prepare the peas ahead of time if you prefer.

In a large bowl, combine the peas, sesame oil, curry powder, yogurt, flour, and salt and pepper to taste, and mash with your hands. Form into 4 to 6 patties.

Although you can bake these (350°F [180°C, or gas mark 4] for 15 minutes per side, covered in a foil tent), do yourself a favor and panfry them in olive oil for 3 to 5 minutes per side, or until a nice crispy, golden brown crust forms. Alternatively, brush with a small amount of olive oil, and use your Air-Fryer at 375°F (190°C) for 14 to 16 minutes.

You Are SO Vegan!

Up the veggies by adding ½ cup (56 g) of finely shredded carrots to the burger dough before forming the patties.

Chapter 5

TOFU-BASED BURGERS

Turn that boring bean curd into beautiful burgers.

THE TRIFECTA BURGER

No-Sugar Added

Soy haters need not apply. The three Ts of soy (TVP, Tofu, and Tempeh) join forces to create a protein-packed burger that will rock your socks off. Serve on a toasted bagel or toasted white bun with a generous schmear of Tangy Tahini Sauce (page 189), lettuce, tomato, and sprouts, as pictured. A big helping of steamed veggies would also complement this nicely.

1 cup (96 g) TVP granules

1 cup (235 ml) vegetable broth

10 ounces (280 g) extra-firm tofu, drained and pressed

4 ounces (112 g) plain soy tempeh

½ cup (112 g) vegan mayonnaise, store-bought or homemade (page 197)

2 tablespoons (34 g) Sriracha sauce

2 tablespoons (30 ml) sesame oil

½ cup (62 g) all-purpose flour

Oil, for frying (optional)

YIELD: 6 BURGERS

In a microwave-safe bowl, mix together the TVP granules and the broth, cover tightly with plastic wrap, and microwave for 5 to 6 minutes. Alternatively, bring the broth to a boil, pour over the TVP granules, cover, and let sit for 10 minutes. Let cool.

In a mixing bowl, crumble the tofu and tempeh. Mix in the reconstituted TVP. Add the mayonnaise, Sriracha sauce, and sesame oil. Mix well.

Slowly knead in the flour until well incorporated and form into 6 patties. Cook as desired.

Bake at 350°F (180°C, or gas mark 4) for 30 minutes, flipping halfway through. Or bake first, then finish off by lightly frying in a smidge of oil until golden and crispy, 2 to 3 minutes on each side.

You Are SO Vegan!

Make it a Quad! Up the soy-osity (and the protein content!) by subbing out half of the flour with plain unsweetened soy milk powder. The milk powder absorbs a lot of liquid, so if your mixture becomes too dry, add in a little water, 1 teaspoon at a time, until you get a good patty-able consistency.

CRAB CAKES

These are the prettiest little patties! I make 'em small, and I fry them in a lot of oil. I like how the carrots kind of imitate the look of crabmeat. I don't serve these on a bun, although I'm sure they'd taste good that way. I just like to serve these on a bed of greens with Aioli Dipping Sauce (page 195).

¼ cup (20 g) hijiki seaweed

2 cups (470 ml) hot water

12 ounces (340 g) extra-firm tofu, drained and pressed

1 can (15 ounces [425 g]) chickpeas, drained and rinsed

1 yellow onion, diced

1 cup (108 g) shredded carrots

1 cup (144 g) vital wheat gluten flour

2 tablespoons (16 g) Old Bay seasoning

Salt and pepper

½ cup (120 ml) soy or coconut milk (optional, for coating)

1 cup (80 g) panko bread crumbs (optional, for coating)

Oil, for frying

YIELD: 15 BURGERS

Place the hijiki in the hot water and let sit for 10 minutes to reconstitute.

While it's soaking, in a mixing bowl, crumble the tofu, and then add the chickpeas, onion, carrots, flour, Old Bay, and salt and pepper to taste. Mix together with your hands, making sure that you mash some of the chickpeas while leaving some of them intact. Make sure, also, that the flour gets mixed in well and that there are no lumps.

Strain the hijiki, reserving the liquid. Add the hijiki to the mixture and mix well. If the mixture needs more moisture, add a little of the reserved hijiki water until you get a nice patty-able consistency.

Refrigerate for at least 20 minutes before forming into 15 crab cake-size patties. Refrigerate the patties for at least 2 to 3 hours before cooking so that the flavor of the hijiki gets well incorporated. Overnight is even better.

If desired, pour the soymilk into a shallow dish and spread the bread crumbs on a plate. Dip each patty into the soymilk, then dredge in the bread crumbs.

Panfry in oil for 3 to 4 minutes per side, until golden and crispy. If you have a deep fryer, now is a great time to use it!

You Are SO Vegan!

Serve these up Po'boy style by placing 2 or 3 of them into a nice crusty baguette dressed with lettuce, tomato, pickles and vegan mayo. Drizzle your favorite hot sauce all over the top.

TOFU 'N' ROOTS BURGER

Nut Free

No-Sugar Added

Bulb fennel is such an underused and underrated ingredient. The sweet savory combos that it can handle are simply limitless. This burger has a mellow, slightly sweet flavor. I like to complement this with some spicy Chipotle Dipping Sauce (page 192) on a toasted bun with a thick slice of red onion.

2 tablespoons (28 g) nondairy butter

1 bulb (5 to 6 ounces [140 to 168 g]) fennel, roughly chopped

1 onion, roughly chopped

12 ounces (340 g) sweet potatoes, peeled and cubed

2 cloves garlic, chopped

Pinch of salt

2 cups (470 ml) water

1 cup (96 g) TVP granules

1 teaspoon cumin

18 ounces (504 g) extra-firm tofu, drained and pressed

½ cup (72 g) vital wheat gluten flour

1 cup (125 g) all-purpose flour

Oil, for frying (optional)

YIELD: 8 TO 10 BURGERS

Preheat the oven to 350°F (180°C, or gas mark 4). Line a baking sheet with parchment or a silicone baking mat.

In a frying pan or skillet, melt the butter over medium-high heat. Add the fennel, onion, sweet potatoes, and garlic. Sprinkle with a pinch of salt. Sauté until just beginning to brown, about 5 minutes.

Add the water, deglaze the pan, and bring to a boil. Lower the heat to a simmer, cover, and simmer for 15 minutes.

Stir in the TVP granules and cumin. Remove from the heat, cover, and let sit for 10 minutes.

Transfer to a large mixing bowl and crumble in the tofu, then add the flours. Knead with your hands until very well incorporated. Let sit for at least 20 minutes to thicken a bit.

Form into 8 to 10 patties and place on the prepared baking sheet. Bake, uncovered, for 30 minutes, or bake for 20 minutes and finish off by panfrying in a bit of oil for about 3 minutes per side. Alternately you can Air-Fry for 14 to 16 minutes at 375°F (190°C).

You Are SO Vegan!

> A green side, such as steamed kale, collards, broccoli, or asparagus, pairs well with the sweet meatiness of this burger.

SCARBOROUGH FAIR TOFU BURGER

Nut Free Gluten-Free No-Oil Added No-Sugar Added

If there was ever a reason to call a veggie burger hippie food, then this burger fits the bill. Inspired by Simon & Garfunkel, these burgers are sure to please your peace-lovin' pals. Normally, I'd advocate for the use of fresh herbs, but for this one, dried works best.

1 tablespoon (2 g) dried parsley

1 tablespoon (2 g) dried sage

1 tablespoon (2 g) dried rosemary

1 tablespoon (2 g) dried thyme

12 ounces (340 g) extra-firm tofu, drained and pressed

1 cup (96 g) TVP granules

1 cup (235 ml) vegetable broth

2 tablespoons (30 g) minced garlic

2½ tablespoons (19 g) ground flaxseed mixed with 3 tablespoons (45 ml) water

¼ cup (32 g) hulled sunflower seeds

¼ cup (32 g) hulled pumpkin seeds

Salt and pepper

YIELD: 6 BURGERS

Grind the parsley, sage, rosemary, and thyme into a fine powder. I use a coffee grinder for this.

In a mixing bowl, crumble the tofu and mix well with the spice mixture so that the herbs are well infused with the tofu. Let sit for the flavors to meld.

In a microwave-safe bowl, mix together the TVP granules and the broth, cover tightly with plastic wrap, and microwave for 5 to 6 minutes. Alternatively, bring the broth to a boil, pour over the TVP, cover, and let sit for 10 minutes.

When cool enough to handle, add the TVP to the tofu mixture, then add the minced garlic, flaxseed mixture, sunflower seeds, pumpkin seeds, and salt and pepper to taste. Mix with your hands until all the ingredients are very well incorporated. Shape into 6 patties. Refrigerate until ready to cook, although refrigeration isn't necessary if you plan on cooking them right away.

I recommend baking these rather than frying. Preheat the oven to 350°F (180°C, or gas mark 4) and line a baking sheet with parchment or a silicone baking mat. Bake, covered with a foil tent, for 15 minutes per side.

You Are SO Vegan!

This one pairs very nicely with a whole grain bun and a light schmear of Creamy Balsamic Dressing (page 195). Sprouts, avocado, and tomato are also good toppings. It's best served with a hearty green salad or steamed veggies.

STRAWBERRY FIELDS BURGER

Nut Free

A few years back I started working at Tanaka Farms in Irvine, California. It's a 30-acre family owned and operated farm in the heart of Orange County. They are known for lots of things, but strawberries are one of their biggest draws. I do many things on the farm, including teaching vegan cooking classes showcasing the farm's produce. This burger is inspired by the farm I now call my office.

FOR THE STRAWBERRY SALSA FRESCA:

1 cup (166 g) chopped ripe strawberries

1 cup (160 g) diced Maui-style or sweet white onion

½ cup (50 g) chopped green onion

½ cup (8 g) chopped cilantro

2 tablespoons (20 g) minced garlic

1 tablespoon (15 ml) lime juice

2 fresh jalapeños, diced, optional

Salt, to taste

FOR THE PATTIES:

1 cup (100 g) TVP granules

1 cup (235 ml) water or vegetable broth

1 cup (235 ml) Strawberry BBQ Sauce (page 191)

1 cup (144 g) vital wheat gluten flour

1 cup (259 g) Strawberry Salsa Fresca (above)

Oil, for frying (optional)

YIELD: 6 BURGERS AND 3 CUPS (777 G) SALSA

To make the strawberry salsa fresca: Add all ingredients to a mixing bowl and mix until well combined.

Keep refrigerated in an airtight container until ready to use. Should last up to 1 week in the refrigerator.

To make the burgers: In a large microwave-safe bowl, mix together the TVP granules and the broth, cover tightly with plastic wrap, and microwave for 5 to 6 minutes. Alternatively, bring the broth to a boil, pour over the TVP granules, cover, and let sit for 10 minutes. Let cool.

Mix in the BBQ sauce, flour, and salsa. Let sit for about 20 minutes to allow the gluten to develop. (You may refrigerate it for later use at this point if you choose.) Divide mixture into 6 equal portions.

Form into patties. Cook as desired. Panfry in oil for 3 to 5 minutes per side over medium-high heat, or until a nice crispy crust forms; Air-Fry at 375°F (190°C) for 16 to 18 minutes; or bake them at 350°F (180°C, or gas mark 4) on a baking sheet lined with parchment or a silicone baking mat, uncovered, for 30 minutes, flipping halfway through. Serve topped with a heaping pile of additional strawberry salsa fresca on top.

You Are SO Vegan!

Make this burger soy and gluten-free by replacing the reconstituted TVP with brown rice and the vital wheat gluten with oat flour.

TOFU "BEEF" PATTY

No-Sugar Added *No-Oil Added*

Nut Free

Super simple and flavorful, these perfectly round beef-y patties make a great substitute for the more labor-intensive beef-y type burgers in chapter 3, especially when making some of the fast food favorites in chapter 10.

1 pound (454 g) super or extra-firm tofu, drained and pressed

½ cup (120 ml) water

½ cup (120 ml) soy sauce or tamari

¼ cup (60 ml) steak sauce

2 tablespoons (16 g) garlic powder

2 tablespoons (16 g) onion powder

½ teaspoon pepper

―――――――

YIELD: 4 BURGERS

Carefully cut the block of tofu into slabs about ¼-inch (6-mm) thick. Using a 4-inch (10-cm) cookie cutter, cut 4 rounds from the slabs. Set aside.

Add remaining ingredients to a resealable bag, or shallow dish with a lid, and mix well. Add tofu rounds to the mixture and marinate for at least 30 minutes, or up to overnight.

Cook as desired. This patty can be baked at 350°F (176°C) for 10 minutes per side, Air-Fried for 12 to 14 minutes at 375°F (190°C), or panfried in a nonstick pan over medium-high heat for about 3 minutes per side, or until warmed all the way through.

You Are SO Vegan!

Freezing tofu before using it in recipes can radically alter the texture . . . in a good way! After cutting your tofu into rounds, arrange them on a baking sheet in a single layer and freeze. Thaw, and gently press out any excess moisture, before placing them into the marinade and notice how the newly transformed tofu sucks up the flavor of the marinade like a sponge and gives it a chewier texture once cooked.

TOFU "CHICKEN" PATTY

No-Sugar Added No-Oil Added

Nut Free

Using the same process as the Tofu "Beef" Patties on the opposite page, these chicken-flavored patties make a fuss-free patty perfect for simple chicken sandwiches on Agave Wheat Buns (page 213) with a schmear of mayo and a crisp piece of romaine lettuce.

1 pound (454 g) super or extra-firm tofu, drained and pressed

1 cup (235 ml) water or low sodium vegetable broth

3 tablespoons (23 g) nutritional yeast

1 tablespoon (2 g) dried parsley

1 tablespoon (8 g) onion powder

1½ teaspoons garlic powder

1 teaspoon celery seed

½ teaspoon salt

½ teaspoon dried oregano

½ teaspoon turmeric

¼ teaspoon thyme

¼ teaspoon dried rosemary

¼ teaspoon black pepper

―――――――――

YIELD: 4 BURGERS

Carefully cut the block of tofu into slabs about ¼-inch (6-mm) thick. Using a 4-inch (10-cm) cookie cutter, cut 4 rounds from the slabs. Set aside.

Add remaining ingredients to a resealable bag, or shallow dish with a lid, and mix well. Add tofu rounds to the mixture and marinate for at least 30 minutes, or up to overnight.

Cook as desired. This patty can be baked at 350°F (176°C) for 10 minutes per side, Air-Fried for 12 to 14 minutes at 375°F (190°C), or panfried in a nonstick pan over medium-high heat for about 3 minutes per side, or until warmed all the way through.

You Are SO Vegan!

Since these ones are so simple, why not add a few steps and turn these into fried chicken patties by following the same method for breading and frying used in the Chicken Fried Steak Burger on page 130.

CURRIED MACADAMIA NUT-CRUSTED TOFU BURGER

No-Oil Added

No-Sugar Added

I first made these burgers after returning home from a week in beautiful Ka'anapali on the island of Maui. I just couldn't get enough macadamia nuts and was making dishes with them daily. I love this burger because it tastes great as a sandwich, served on a toasted bun with a schmear of Indian-Spiced Mayo (page 192), but also works great as a main dish, sans the bun.

12 ounces (340 g) extra-firm tofu, drained and pressed

1 cup (115 g) panko bread crumbs

2 tablespoons (12 g) yellow curry powder

⅓ cup (44 g) chopped dry-roasted macadamia nuts

1 teaspoon paprika

¼ teaspoon sea salt

¼ teaspoon freshly cracked black pepper

1 can (14 ounces [425 ml]) full-fat coconut milk

YIELD: 4 BURGERS

Preheat the oven to 350°F (180°C, or gas mark 4). Line a baking sheet with parchment or a silicone mat, or spray with cooking spray.

Carefully cut the tofu into 4 equal "steaks." (You can use a round cookie cutter if you are ethically opposed to square burgers. *I see you.*)

In a shallow dish, combine the bread crumbs, curry powder, nuts, paprika, salt, and pepper. Pour the coconut milk into a separate shallow dish.

Dip the tofu into the coconut milk, and then dredge in the bread crumb mixture to coat. Repeat with the other 3 pieces and place on the prepared baking sheet.

Bake for about 30 minutes, or until firm and just beginning to brown.

You Are SO Vegan!

Seriously? You just made *Curried Macadamia Nut-Crusted Tofu Burgers.* You don't think this is vegan enough?

CHOW MEIN BURGER

You can add all kinds of veggies to this one. I stuck with carrots and broccoli, but baby corn, edamame, red bell peppers, mung bean sprouts, sugar snap peas, or whatever else you have on hand would make a great addition to the recipe. Serve piping hot, topped with extra chow mein noodles, and sprinkled with a few sesame seeds over a bed of steamed cabbage with a dollop of Chinese hot mustard, hot ketchup, or Sriracha for dipping.

1 package (6 ounces [170 g]) chow mein noodles

2 tablespoons (30 ml) sesame oil

8 ounces (227 g) broccoli florets

1 cup (108 g) sliced or shredded carrots

½ cup (65 g) raw cashew pieces

1 tablespoon (6 g) grated fresh ginger

2 tablespoons (30 ml) peanut oil

12 ounces (340 g) extra-firm tofu, drained, pressed, and cut into small cubes

¼ cup (60 ml) soy sauce or tamari

1 tablespoon (8 g) sesame seeds

½ cup (128 g) cashew nut butter

¼ cup (32 g) potato starch or cornstarch

Salt and pepper

Oil, for frying

YIELD: 6 BURGERS

Prepare the noodles according to the package instructions. Drain, divide into 2 equal portions, and set aside.

Using a wok or a large frying pan, heat the sesame oil. Add the broccoli, carrots, cashew pieces, and ginger. Stir-fry for 5 to 7 minutes. Add the peanut oil, then the tofu. Continue to cook 5 more minutes, tossing often. Add the soy sauce, half of the noodles, and the sesame seeds. Toss to coat and continue to cook 5 minutes longer.

Turn off the heat and add the cashew butter, stirring to coat. Let cool.

Sprinkle in the potato starch and, using your hands, knead together. Season with salt and pepper.

Form into 6 patties. Line a plate with paper towels.

Preheat ¼ inch (6 mm) oil in a frying pan over high heat. The oil is ready when a piece of dough dropped into it sizzles immediately.

Fry the patties for about 5 minutes per side, until a nice crispy, golden brown crust forms. Transfer to the plate to drain excess oil.

Serve with the remaining half of the chow mein noodles.

You Are SO Vegan!

To make this gluten-free opt for Shirataki noodles and choose gluten-free tamari.

Chapter 6

GRAIN-BASED BURGERS

From oats, to barley, to corn, to rice, these hearty burgers are sure to play nice!

BEEF AND BROCCOLI BURGER

These are like a bowl from one of those take-out joints, but in the shape of a burger! A caveat: I make these ones really big and really, really chunky. I like 'em that way. You can certainly improve the stability of your burgers, especially if you want to serve them on a bun, by simply placing all of the ingredients in a food processor and pulsing a few times before forming into patties. I don't think these need a bun. I like to serve mine with the typical take-out-style sides.

1 pound (454 g) prepared seitan, store-bought or homemade (page 203), chopped into small pieces

8 ounces (227 g) broccoli florets, chopped to the size of your liking

2 cups (348 g) cooked sushi rice or plain white rice

½ cup (62 g) all-purpose or ½ cup (80 g) rice flour

½ cup (120 ml) teriyaki sauce

1 tablespoon (15 ml) rice vinegar

1 tablespoon (8 g) sesame seeds

YIELD: 4 GIANT BURGERS OR 6 HUMAN-SIZE ONES

In a mixing bowl, combine the seitan, broccoli, rice, and flour. Knead to combine. This is a very sticky mixture.

Form into 4 to 6 patties and set aside.

Whisk together the teriyaki sauce, vinegar, and sesame seeds. Pour into a large nonstick pan and bring to a simmer.

Place the patties in the pan, simmer for 5 to 7 minutes, flip and cook 5 minutes longer. The patties will absorb most, if not all, of the liquid.

You Are SO Vegan!

Swap out the white rice for brown rice and serve over a bed of steamed cabbage.

KASHA BURGER

No-Sugar Added

Nut Free

Kasha is a traditional porridge enjoyed in Eastern Europe. In Jewish cuisine, the addition of bow-tie pasta and brown gravy makes it kasha varnishkes. I thought bow ties were a little big for burgers, so I replaced them with couscous. Serve this burger open-faced on grilled sourdough topped with brown gravy.

2 tablespoons (28 g) nondairy butter, plus extra for frying (optional)

½ cup (82 g) buckwheat groats (kasha)

1 onion, diced

2 cups (470 ml) vegetable broth

¾ cup (130 g) dried couscous

½ cup (60 g) rye flour

Salt and pepper

YIELD: 5 TO 6 BURGERS

In a large skillet or pot, melt the 2 tablespoons (28 g) butter over medium heat. Add the buckwheat groats and cook for about 2 minutes, stirring constantly. Add the onions and continue to cook and stir for about 5 minutes longer. Add the broth. Bring to a boil, lower the heat to a simmer, cover, and cook for 10 minutes. Stir in the couscous, remove from the heat, cover, and allow the couscous to absorb the moisture. Stir well and let cool.

Preheat the oven to 350°F (180°C, or gas mark 4). Line a baking sheet with parchment or a silicone baking mat.

Add the rye flour and salt and pepper to taste, and knead until a patty-able consistency is reached. Form into 5 or 6 patties. Cook as desired.

Panfry in additional butter over medium heat for 3 to 4 minutes per side, or until golden and crispy, Alternatively, use your Air-Fryer at 375°F (190°C) for 16 to 18 minutes. You can also bake these at 350°F (180°C, or gas mark 4), uncovered, on a baking sheet lined with parchment or a silicone baking mat, for 10 minutes, and then flip and bake for 10 minutes longer, until firm and just beginning to brown.

You Are SO Vegan!

Make a quick and dirty brown gravy by heating ¼ cup (60 ml) oil over medium heat. Add in ¼ cup (31 g) all-purpose flour and stir to combine to make a roux. Continue to stir and cook until golden. Add in 2 cups (470 ml) beef-flavored vegetable broth and stir to mix completely. Add in 2 tablespoons (15 g) nutritional yeast, and salt and pepper to taste. Continue to stir until thickened. It should only take a few minutes. Keep warm until ready to serve.

THIS BURGER IS NUTS!

Protein-packed and full of earthy nutty flavor, this burger stands up well to many types of cuisine, so feel free to dress it up as you wish, or in other words . . . go nuts!

Soy-Free

No-Sugar Added

---

2 tablespoons (30 ml) olive oil, plus more for frying (optional)

8 ounces (227 g) mushrooms, sliced or chopped

3 cloves garlic, minced

¾ cup (180 ml) vegetable broth

1 cup (100 g) prepared brown rice

¼ cup (28 g) cashews, chopped

¼ cup (32 g) sunflower seeds

¼ cup (27 g) pecans, chopped

¼ cup (30 g) walnuts, chopped

¼ cup (30 g) nutritional yeast

½ cup (72 g) vital wheat gluten flour

1 tablespoon (8 g) ground mustard

1 tablespoon (8 g) onion powder

1 teaspoon liquid smoke (optional)

Salt and pepper, to taste

YIELD: 4 BURGERS (½ POUND [227 G]) OR 8 BURGERS (¼ POUND [114 G])

In a heavy-bottom skillet, heat the oil and sauté the mushrooms and garlic for 5 to 7 minutes, or until fragrant and beginning to brown. Add the vegetable broth and bring to a simmer. Add the rice, nuts, and seeds. Mix well, cover, and remove from the heat. Let sit for 10 minutes.

When cool enough to handle, add the nutritional yeast, gluten flour, ground mustard, onion powder, and liquid smoke, if using. Add salt and pepper to taste. Mix well using your hands.

Place in the fridge to cool for about 20 minutes. This will help the dough stiffen up a bit. Form into 4 to 8 patties, depending on size preference.

Preheat oven to 350°F (180°C, or gas mark 4). Line a baking sheet with parchment, or a reusable silicon baking mat. Arrange patties on the mat, and bake for 25 minutes. Flip and bake an additional 15 minutes. Alternatively, you can panfry these burgers in a bit of oil for 4 to 5 minutes per side until crispy and golden.

You Are SO Vegan!

To make this recipe gluten-free, substitute ½ cup (40 g) finely ground quick-cooking oats for the vital wheat gluten.

SAVORY NOODLE KUGEL BURGER

Let me start off by saying that I am not Jewish, and I make no claims to the authenticity or kosherness of this kugel burger. I do know that this is certainly not acceptable for Passover, but it might be okay for Chanukah. What I will stand by, however, is the cheesy goodness of, what is to me, mac and cheeze on a bun. Warning: This is not low fat, this is not low cal, this is not health food in any sense of the word. What it is? Pure rich and delicious decadence.

8 ounces (227 g) uncooked macaroni

2 cups (220 g) shredded potatoes

12 ounces (340 g) extra-firm tofu, drained, pressed, and crumbled to resemble ricotta

¼ cup (60 g) nondairy cream cheese

¼ cup (56 g) nondairy butter

¼ cup (30 g) nutritional yeast

¼ cup (65 g) raw cashews, ground into a fine powder

1 tablespoon (8 g) onion powder

1 tablespoon (8 g) garlic powder

1 tablespoon (18 g) white miso

Pinch of paprika

Salt and pepper

1 cup (115 g) crushed cornflakes or bread crumbs

Oil, for frying (optional)

YIELD: 8 BURGERS

Cook the macaroni in salted water according to the package instructions.

While the macaroni is cooking, in a large mixing bowl, combine the potatoes, tofu, cream cheese, butter, yeast, cashew powder, onion powder, garlic powder, miso, paprika, and salt and pepper to taste. Using your hands, mash everything together until well combined and uniform.

Add the drained, cooked macaroni noodles, and mash again until well incorporated. Finally, mash in the cornflakes.

Form into 8 patties. Cook as desired.

Panfry in plenty of oil over medium heat for 5 minutes per side, or until golden and crispy; Air-Fry at 375°F (190°C) for 18 to 20 minutes; or bake at 350°F (180°C, or gas mark 4), uncovered, on a baking sheet lined with parchment or a silicone baking mat, for about 15 minutes, and then flip and bake for 15 minutes longer, until firm and just beginning to brown.

You Are SO Vegan!

Not in the mood for burgers? Pack this mixture into a square baking dish and serve it as a casserole. Just bake it, uncovered, at 350°F (180°C, or gas mark 4) for 15 to 20 minutes, or until the top is golden and crispy.

POPEYE BURGER

Gluten-Free *No-Sugar Added* *Soy-Free*

Eat your spinach and you will be strong! I really think the Popeye cartoons were on to something, you know? The Sun-Dried Tomato Aioli (page 193) makes a tasty spread on these. Strangely enough, I also like these alongside mashed potatoes. Go figure!

2 cups (380 g) uncooked brown rice

1 can (14 ounces [392 g]) spinach

1 cup (80 g) quick-cooking oats

½ cup (68 g) raw or toasted pine nuts

1 tablespoon (8 g) garlic powder

1 tablespoon (8 g) onion powder

1 tablespoon (8 g) ground mustard

1 teaspoon dried basil

1 teaspoon sweet paprika

3 tablespoons (45 ml) sesame oil

Salt and pepper

Oil, for frying (optional)

————

YIELD: 8 BURGERS

Prepare the rice in a rice cooker or on the stove according to package directions.

Drain the excess liquid from the spinach and place in a mixing bowl with the oats; let sit while the rice is cooking. The oats will absorb the moisture from the spinach and soften.

When the rice is fully cooked, mix it into the spinach mixture and add the pine nuts, garlic powder, onion powder, mustard, basil, paprika, oil, and salt and pepper to taste.

When it is cool enough to handle, form into 8 patties.

Panfry in a little oil, about 3 to 5 minutes per side until golden and crispy; Air-Fry at 375°F (190°C) for 14 to 16 minutes; or bake at 350°F (180°C, or gas mark 4) for 15 minutes per side, covered loosely in foil, until firm and warmed all the way through. Or grill wrapped in foil to prevent breakage, for about 20 minutes, until firm and warmed all the way through.

You Are SO Vegan!

Replace the sesame oil with Olive Oyl (see what I did there?) and add 1 teaspoon (or more if you like it extra spicy) red chili flakes. Serve topped with fire roasted jalapeños to prove you're no Wimpy. (Oh Jeep-ers, that was really bad!)

JALAPEÑO CORNBREAD BURGER

Nut Free

Cornbread meets burger, and it's getting pretty spicy. Garnish with Nacho Cheesy Sauce (page 188) and more jalapeños. Nondairy Sour Cream (page 198) is a nice garnish to cool it down a bit.

1 cup (96 g) **TVP granules**

2 tablespoons (16 g) **taco seasoning,** store-bought or homemade (page 201)

1 tablespoon (8 g) **cumin**

1 scant cup (225 ml) **water**

1 cup (140 g) **yellow cornmeal**

16 to 20 slices **jarred or canned jalapeños,** diced

¼ cup (60 ml) **juice from jar of jalapeños**

¼ cup (60 ml) **vegetable oil,** plus more for frying (optional)

¼ cup (31 g) **all-purpose flour**

1 cup (160 g) **diced white or yellow onion**

½ cup (125 g) **yellow corn kernels**

¼ cup (40 g) **diced red bell pepper** (optional)

Salt and pepper

YIELD: 6 BURGERS

In a microwave-safe bowl, mix together the TVP granules, taco seasoning, cumin, and water. Cover tightly with plastic wrap and microwave for 5 to 6 minutes. Or, bring the water to a boil, pour over the TVP granules and spices, cover, and let sit for 10 minutes. Let cool.

Add the cornmeal, jalapeños, jalapeño juice, the ¼ cup (60 ml) oil, flour, onion, corn, bell pepper, if using, and salt and pepper to taste. Knead thoroughly until all the cornmeal and flour are absorbed into the mix. Refrigerate for about 20 minutes.

Form into 6 patties and cook as desired.

To grill, wrap them loosely in foil and grill for about 20 minutes. It effectively steams itself inside the foil. Or, fry in oil until golden and crispy, 3 to 5 minutes per side. Or, bake in the oven at 350°F (180°C, or gas mark 4), on a baking sheet lined with parchment or a silicone baking mat, loosely covered in foil, for 25 to 30 minutes, flipping halfway through.

You Are SO Vegan!

Serve open-faced as a Jalapeño Cornbread Chili Burger by topping with your favorite vegan chili or the chili from Three Bean Chili Burger on page 63.

INSIDE-OUT SUSHI BURGER

Gluten-Free

Nut Free

This fun take on sushi is definitely a looker! The black-and-white sesame seeds make it so pretty, and the little wrap of nori is a nod to the handheld snacks known as Sweet Potato Mochi (Japanese Sweet Potato Pancakes). These are served cold, which makes them a great make-ahead dish. You can make the components ahead of time, so all you have to do is assemble at burger time. Serve with Creamy Sesame Sriracha Sauce (page 200) for dipping.

FOR THE SWEET RICE:

2 cups (360 g) sushi rice

3 ¾ cups (885 ml) water

2 tablespoons (30 ml) rice vinegar

2 tablespoons (30 ml) agave

½ teaspoon salt

FOR THE WATERMELON TUNA:

¼ cup (60 ml) rice vinegar

2 tablespoons (30 ml) toasted sesame oil

2 tablespoons (30 ml) gluten-free tamari

1 tablespoon (15 ml) balsamic vinegar

12 pieces red, seedless watermelon cut into strips about 2 inches (5 cm) long by ¼ inch (6-mm) thick by 1 inch (2.5 cm) wide

To make the sweet rice: Throw all ingredients into your rice cooker, give it a stir to combine, and press start. If you do not have a rice cooker, follow the directions on the package of rice, adding the vinegar, agave, and salt to the water. Once cooked, chill until ready to make the burgers.

To make the watermelon tuna: Mix together all ingredients except watermelon in a shallow dish with a lid, or a re-sealable plastic bag. Add watermelon and refrigerate for at least 1 hour, but it's even better if you can do it overnight.

Transfer marinated watermelon to a pan with a lid. Cook covered on medium-high heat for 20 to 30 minutes, stirring occasionally.

Remove the lid and continue cooking for about 10 minutes more, or until deep red and translucent. Drain off any excess liquid. Chill until ready to assemble your burgers.

FOR THE BURGERS:

Sweet rice (opposite page)

Watermelon Tuna (opposite page)

12 pieces of green onion cut into
2½-inch (6.3-cm) pieces

6 cucumber slices cut lengthwise into
2 ½-inch (6.3-cm) pieces

⅓ cup (36 g) shredded carrots

1 ripe, but firm, avocado, sliced
lengthwise into 12 slices

2 nori sheets cut into 6 rectangles
measuring 2 inches (5 cm) by
5 inches (12.5 cm)

¼ cup (32 g) black sesame seeds

¼ cup (32 g) white sesame seeds

YIELD: 6 BURGERS

To make the burgers: Line a cutting board with plastic wrap or work on a nonstick silicone mat. Have a small dish of water at the ready to rinse your fingers as you work. (That rice is sticky!) Have all of your ingredients at the ready to make assembly easy.

Measure ¾ cup (118 g) rice and place on the mat. Dived in half and form each half into a patty shape. If you have enough space on your mat, you can form all of the rice patties and fill all of the patties at the same time. (If you are like me, your space isn't that big, so you may have to do one at a time.) All together you will have 12 patties that will yield 6 burgers.

Arrange 2 slices watermelon tuna, 2 pieces of green onion, 1 piece of cucumber, about 2 tablespoons (14 g) carrots, and 2 avocado slices in the center of one patty. Top with another patty and press the edges together to seal.

Place the short end of the rectangle of nori at the center of the burger and wrap around to the bottom of the burger, and press to stick to the rice. If it does not stick, use a little water to help it adhere to the rice.

Place sesame seeds in a shallow dish. Place the burger in the seeds to coat. The seeds will not stick to the nori.

Serve chilled.

You Are SO Vegan!

Too much effort? Just make sushi burritos instead! Use a whole sheet of nori for the "tortilla" and spread with rice. Layer all other ingredients inside, sprinkle with sesame seeds, and roll it up!

PINTOS AND RICE BURGER

Soy-Free

Nut-Free

No-Sugar Added

This one couldn't be simpler. Simply mush all the ingredients together and bake or fry. I'd be lying if I told you I didn't like it better fried, but baked tastes delicious too, and is certainly better for the waistline.

1 can (15 ounces [425 g]) pinto beans, drained

2 cups (330 g) cooked brown or white rice

1 cup (180 g) diced tomatoes

1 cup (160 g) diced onion

½ cup (70 g) yellow cornmeal

½ cup (62 g) all-purpose flour

1 jalapeño pepper, seeded if desired, and diced

1 tablespoon (15 g) minced garlic

1 teaspoon hot sauce (I like Tabasco or Tapatío)

½ teaspoon ground cumin

Salt and pepper

Oil, for frying (optional)

YIELD: 8 BURGERS

In a mixing bowl, combine all the ingredients and knead with your hands.

Form into 8 patties and cook as desired.

Panfry in plenty of oil for 4 to 5 minutes per side, until golden and crispy; Air-Fry at 375°F (190°C) for 16 to 18 minutes; or bake, uncovered, at 350°F (180°C, or gas mark 4) for 15 minutes on a baking sheet lined with parchment or a silicone baking mat, and then flip and bake for 15 minutes longer, until firm and just beginning to brown.

You Are SO Vegan!

I like this one a couple of ways: as a burger, on a toasted bun smothered with guacamole and topped with a few slices of jalapeños; served up with a big old side of chips and salsa or a grilled ear of corn on the cob (as shown here); or sandwiched in a flour tortilla and grilled quesadilla style, with some Nacho Cheesy Sauce (page 188), guacamole, and Nondairy Sour Cream (page 198).

SARAH'S SOUTHWEST BURGER

Nut Free

No-Sugar Added

This recipe yields eight whoppin' burgers, so unless you plan on feeding lots of hungry veganos, feel free to cut the recipe in half, or freeze the patties for quick dinners throughout the week. Serve on a nice hearty bun with a schmear of Nondairy Sour Cream (page 198) and some salsa. Serve with tortilla chips and Cilantro Lime Rice (page 227).

1 cup (96 g) TVP granules

1 cup (235 ml) vegetable broth or water

1 can (15 ounces [425 g]) black beans, drained

2 cups (280 g) canned, fresh, or frozen corn kernels

2 cups (330 g) cooked brown rice

1 heaping cup (190 g) diced tomatoes, drained

½ cup (80 g) finely diced onion

¼ cup (40 g) finely diced jarred jalapeños (optional)

3 tablespoons (45 ml) canola oil

1 cup (144 g) vital wheat gluten flour

¼ cup (32 g) cornstarch

2 tablespoons (16 g) garlic powder

2 tablespoons (16 g) onion powder

1 teaspoon unsweetened cocoa powder

1 teaspoon paprika

Salt and pepper

_____

YIELD: 8 BURGERS

In a microwave-safe bowl, mix together the TVP granules and broth, cover tightly with plastic wrap, and microwave for 5 to 6 minutes. Alternatively, bring the broth to a boil, pour over the TVP granules, cover, and let sit for 10 minutes. Let cool.

In a mixing bowl, combine the beans, corn, cooked rice, tomatoes, onion, jalapeños, and oil. In a separate bowl, mix together the flour, cornstarch, garlic powder, onion powder, cocoa, paprika, and salt and pepper to taste.

When cool enough to handle, combine the reconstituted TVP with the rice and veggie mixture. Mix well with your hands so that the beans and rice start to get mushed in pretty well with the TVP. Add the flour and spice mixture, and knead for a few minutes until a nice dough forms. Place the mixture in the refrigerator for at least 30 minutes to rest.

Preheat the oven to 350°F (180°C, or gas mark 4). Line a baking sheet with parchment or a silicone baking mat.

Form into 8 patties, place on the prepared baking sheet, and bake, uncovered, for 15 minutes, then flip and bake for 15 minutes longer, until firm and just beginning to brown.

You Are SO Vegan!

Serve these up Torta style by using bolillo or telera rolls in place of buns. Spread one side of the roll with a thick layer of guacamole, and the other with vegan sour cream. Add the patty and shredded lettuce. Garnish with pico de gallo.

COUSCOUS PANTRY BURGER

Nut Free

No-Sugar Added

The reason these are called pantry burgers is because I developed this recipe as I was conducting "The Great Grocery Experiment" inspired by my cousin, Leah, and her husband, Tim. I set out to go a month without buying any food, using only what I already had in my kitchen. Each time I created a new and noteworthy dish, I dubbed it a "pantry" dish. And if only for this burger alone, it was a worthwhile experiment! If you like vegan cheeses, a slice of vegan mozzarella would work well here. Also, top with some roasted garlic or Aioli Dipping Sauce (page 195). A bit of Chunky Marinara (page 194) would be tasty, too. Fried Zucchini (page 217) would be a perfect side dish with these. The perfect bun? Try the Rustica Bun (page 209).

2 cups (470 ml) vegetable broth

1 can (14 ounces [392 g]) tomato sauce

1 cup (174 g) dry couscous

1 cup (96 g) TVP granules

1 tablespoon (2 g) dried basil or 3 tablespoons (9 g) fresh, finely chopped

2 tablespoons (30 g) minced garlic

¼ cup (31 g) shredded or grated zucchini

2 tablespoons (19 g) ground flaxseed mixed with 3 tablespoons (45 ml) warm water

1 cup (120 g) whole wheat pastry flour

¼ cup (30 g) nutritional yeast

2 tablespoons (30 ml) olive oil, plus extra for frying

YIELD: 8 BURGERS

Bring the vegetable broth and tomato sauce to a boil. Lower the heat to a simmer.

Add the couscous and TVP, stir well, cover, and remove from the heat. Let sit for 10 minutes to absorb all of the liquid.

When cool enough to handle, add the basil, garlic, zucchini, flaxseed mixture, flour, nutritional yeast, and 2 tablespoons (30 ml) oil. Mix together and knead so that all ingredients are well incorporated and a nice patty-able consistency is reached.

Form into 8 patties and fry in oil for 3 to 5 minutes per side, until golden and crispy. I don't recommend baking or Air-Frying these because they will get too dried out.

You Are SO Vegan!

The next time you think to yourself, "There's nothing to eat!" as you stare in your cupboards, challenge yourself to your own *Great Grocery Experiment*! You might be surprised at what you come up with!

CHINESE TAKE-OUT BURGER

Nut Free

This burger is super fun to make and the additions and substitutions you can make are only limited by your imagination. Here is the basic recipe with suggestions for optional add-ins. I use white rice for a base because sticky white rice is what I think of when I think of Chinese take-out. However, you can use brown rice instead. No bun required on this one!

FOR GLAZE:

1½ cups (355 ml) water

2 tablespoons (30 ml) orange juice

¼ cup (60 ml) lemon juice

⅓ cup (80 ml) rice vinegar (in a pinch you can use 2 tablespoons [30 ml] apple cider vinegar)

2½ tablespoons (38 ml) soy sauce

1 tablespoon (6 g) grated orange zest or 1 teaspoon orange extract

1 cup (225 g) firmly packed brown sugar

½ teaspoon freshly minced ginger-root or ¼ teaspoon ground

1 teaspoon minced garlic

½ teaspoon red pepper flakes

3 tablespoons (24 g) cornstarch dissolved in 2 tablespoons (30 ml) water to make a slurry

To make the glaze: Combine all the glaze ingredients, except for the cornstarch slurry, in a saucepan and bring to a boil, stirring occasionally. Reduce to a simmer and slowly add the cornstarch mixture; continue to stir as it thickens. Lower the heat to keep warm and reserve.

FOR PATTIES:

2 cups (348 g) fully cooked white rice (you can use any rice you want to, really!)

8 ounces (227 g) plain soy tempeh, crumbled almost into individual beans

½ cup (60 g) chickpea flour (you can probably use plain old all-purpose here too, but I like the flavor of the chickpea flour)

1 tablespoon (6 g) orange zest or 1 teaspoon orange extract

Add-ins (optional): peas, grated carrots, chopped broccoli, diced red peppers, chopped scallions (you know, the stuff you would find in Chinese take-out fried rice!)

FOR COATING:

1 cup (120 g) chickpea flour

½ cup (120 ml) nondairy milk

1 cup (115 g) panko-style bread crumbs

Oil, for frying

YIELD: 5 OR 6 BURGERS

To make the patties: Mix together all the ingredients, using your hands. Squeeze and knead until it becomes very sticky. Form into 5 or 6 patties.

To make the coating: Combine the flour and milk in a bowl. Spread the bread crumbs on a shallow plate. Heat the oil in a frying pan over medium-high heat.

Coat each patty with the flour and milk mixture, and then dredge in the bread crumbs. Place in the frying pan and fry until golden and crispy on each side, 3 to 5 minutes per side. Remove from the oil and dip into the glaze to generously coat both sides.

You Are SO Vegan!

Serve up with a side of grilled bok choy. Take a full head of bok choy and slice in half lengthwise. Brush with olive oil and place cut side down on a hot grill or grill pan. Cook for just a few minutes until grill marks are present and leaves begin to wilt. Sprinkle with sesame seeds and serve.

SUPER QUINOA BURGER

Gluten-Free Soy-Free No-Sugar Added

Since quinoa is the super grain, I shall dub these Super Burgers! I like buns, but this one really tastes good on lettuce. Red leaf is my favorite. A nice big leaf, topped with the patty, some alfalfa sprouts, and drizzled with Tangy Tahini Sauce (page 189, and pictured here). So yum. Brown rice makes a good side dish.

1½ cups (355 ml) vegetable broth

1 cup (173 g) uncooked quinoa

1 can (15 ounces [425 g]) cannellini or navy beans, rinsed and drained

2 cups (300 g) fresh or frozen green peas

½ cup (65 g) raw cashews, ground into a fine powder

1 teaspoon green curry paste

1 teaspoon ground ginger

2 tablespoons (32 g) tahini paste

2 tablespoons (30 ml) sesame oil

½ cup (64 g) cornstarch

Salt and pepper

Oil, for frying

YIELD: 8 BURGERS

Bring the vegetable broth to a boil.

Meanwhile, in a dry pan, heat the uncooked quinoa until it begins to pop (this will happen fairly quickly).

Add the quinoa to the broth, and lower the heat to medium. Cover and cook for 12 minutes, or until all of the broth is absorbed. Remove from the heat, fluff with a fork, and let sit, uncovered, to cool.

In a large mixing bowl, combine the beans, peas, cashew powder, curry, ginger, tahini, and sesame oil. Gently mush the peas and beans, but don't completely mash; chunky is good.

When the quinoa is cooled, fold it into the mixture and add the cornstarch and salt and pepper to taste. Mix well using your hands.

Refrigerate for at least 20 minutes to thicken up a bit before forming into 8 patties.

Panfry in a smidge of oil in a pan until golden on each side, about 3 minutes per side. These taste best panfried. The oven makes them too dry, and they won't hold up well on a grill.

You Are SO Vegan!

These have a wonderful flavor, and I will surely admit to eating the mixture right from the bowl (minus the cornstarch) before I make the patties. In fact, it wouldn't make a bad side dish just as is. Plop a scoop on a plate next to a main dish and done.

Chapter 7

VEGETABLE-BASED BURGERS

I mean, they are called "veggie burgers" for a reason, am I right?

EARTH BURGER

Nut Free   No-Sugar Added

These chunky, hearty, earthy burgers certainly qualify as hippie food. But, seriously, who doesn't love a hippie?

4 ounces (112 g) mushrooms, chopped

3 cloves garlic, minced

¼ cup (60 ml) olive oil, divided

2 cups (330 g) cooked wild rice blend

½ cup (75 g) corn kernels

1½ cups (107 g) chopped broccoli florets

1 cup (144 g) vital wheat gluten flour

½ cup (56 g) soy flour

½ cup (120 ml) water

Salt and pepper

YIELD: 8 BURGERS

Sauté the mushrooms and garlic in 2 tablespoons (30 ml) of the olive oil for 5 to 7 minutes, or until fragrant and beginning to brown.

In a mixing bowl, combine the sautéed mushrooms and garlic, the remaining 2 tablespoons (30 ml) olive oil, rice, corn, broccoli, flours, water, and salt and pepper to taste. Refrigerate for at least 20 minutes to thicken a bit.

Preheat the oven to 375°F (190°C, or gas mark 5). Line a baking sheet with parchment or a silicone baking mat.

Form into 8 patties and place on the prepared baking sheet.

Bake for 25 minutes, uncovered, or until slightly firm and just beginning to brown.

You Are SO Vegan!

Serve with sprouts, avocado, onions, tomatoes, or whatever your heart desires. Serve with a hearty garden salad topped with sunflower seeds and Creamy Balsamic Dressing (page 195) to really make it a hippie meal.

CHIPOTLE SWEET POTATO BURGER

No-Oil Added

Something about the sweetness of a sweet potato combined with the smoky spiciness of chipotle chiles has always reminded me of fall. For this burger, I didn't even need a bun to enjoy the savory with the sweet and just a hint of autumn peeking through.

---

1 large or 2 small sweet potatoes

1 can (7 ounces [195 g]) chipotle chiles in adobo sauce, or less to taste

12 ounces (340 g) extra-firm tofu, drained, pressed, and crumbled

¼ cup (32 g) ground raw cashews

¼ cup (55 g) firmly packed brown sugar

½ teaspoon sea salt

Pinch of nutmeg

Pinch of cinnamon

½ to 1 cup (60 to 120 g) whole wheat pastry flour

YIELD: 8 BURGERS

Preheat the oven to 350°F (180°C, or gas mark 4).

Bake the sweet potatoes with the skin on, directly on the rack, for approximately 45 minutes, or until tender. Remove from the oven and let cool.

When cool, remove the skin (it should come right off) and smash the potato. Measure 2 cups (450 g) smashed sweet potato.

In a mixing bowl, place the potatoes, chipotles, tofu, ground cashews, brown sugar, salt, nutmeg, and cinnamon and mush together really well with your hands. The chipotles should break apart easily as you do this. After everything is well incorporated, add the flour, a little bit at a time.

Depending on the moisture content of your potato and tofu, you'll need just a little or a lot. Refrigerate for 10 to 20 minutes.

Preheat the oven again to 350°F (180°C, or gas mark 4). Line a baking sheet with parchment or a silicone baking mat.

Form into 8 hearty patties and place on the prepared baking sheet.

Bake for 20 minutes, uncovered, then flip and bake for 20 minutes longer, until firm and just beginning to brown.

You Are SO Vegan!

Make the patties on the smallish side, and serve as an appetizer on a bed of greens with Chipotle Dipping Sauce (page 192).

GREEN BEAN ALMONDINE BURGER

Serve this patty as a nontraditional, traditional side at any holiday party you head to, and I guarantee the guests will rejoice. Serve on a toasted piece of French bread or with a schmear of vegan mayo, topped with extra almondine.

FOR ALMONDINE:

3 cups (705 ml) water

1 pound (454 g) fresh green beans, ends trimmed

2 tablespoons (28 g) nondairy butter

8 ounces (227 g) mushrooms, sliced

1 cup (160 g) diced onion

2 tablespoons (30 g) minced garlic

Salt and pepper

¼ cup (27 g) slivered or sliced almonds

¼ cup (25 g) imitation bacon bits, store-bought or homemade (optional, page 201)

FOR BURGERS:

1 recipe Almondine, divided

¼ cup (64 g) almond butter

½ cup (62 g) all-purpose flour

½ cup (72 g) vital wheat gluten flour

Salt and pepper

YIELD: 4 BURGERS

To make the almondine: In your largest frying pan, add the water and bring to a boil (you can add a pinch of salt to the water if you choose). Add the beans and boil for 3 minutes. Remove from the heat, drain, and set aside.

Dry the pan and add the butter. Melt the butter over high heat. Add the mushrooms, onion, and garlic. Sauté until the mushrooms have reduced in size by half, about 7 minutes. Season with salt and pepper. Add the almonds and bacon bits. Cook for 2 minutes longer. Add the green beans. Toss to coat, and cook for 3 to 5 minutes longer.

To make the burgers: Divide the Almondine recipe in half. Set half aside.

Place half the Almondine in the food processor along with the almond butter, flours, and salt and pepper to taste. Pulse until crumbly.

Form into 4 patties and bake. Place on a baking sheet lined with parchment or a silicone mat, cover with foil, and bake at 350°F (180°C, or gas mark 4) for 15 minutes, and then flip and bake 15 minutes longer.

Top with the reserved almondine.

You Are SO Vegan!

The green bean almondine portion of this recipe is a perfect holiday side dish to bring to share at a family dinner. It doesn't "look weird" and it tastes great!

MIND YOUR PEAS AND 'QUES

Nut Free

Yeah, I know, one doesn't normally think of peas and barbecue sauce together, but believe me when I tell you that it really works! Serve on a nice Soft White Bun (page 206) with Creamy BBQ Coleslaw (page 227) piled on top or on the side.

¾ cup (180 ml) vegetable broth

½ cup (136 g) barbecue sauce, store-bought or homemade (page 190)

1 yellow onion, diced

2 cloves garlic, minced

2 tablespoons (30 g) horseradish

2 tablespoons (30 g) Dijon mustard

1 tablespoon (6 g) freshly ground black pepper

1 pound (454 g) fresh or frozen peas

¼ cup (60 ml) olive oil

1 cup (144 g) vital wheat gluten flour

½ cup (60 g) whole wheat flour

Salt

Oil, for frying (optional)

———————

YIELD: 4 TO 6 BURGERS

In a stockpot, bring the broth and barbecue sauce to a boil. Lower the heat to a simmer.

Add the onion and garlic, cover, and cook over medium-low heat for about 20 minutes, or until soft and most of the liquid has been absorbed.

Stir in the horseradish, mustard, pepper, and peas. Heat through. Transfer to a food processor or blender, or use an immersion blender to purée until smooth, but still a bit chunky.

Transfer to a mixing bowl. Stir in the olive oil. Let cool.

Slowly add the flours, season with salt, and knead until a nice patty-able consistency is reached.

Form into 4 to 6 patties and cook as desired. Fry in oil until golden and crispy, 3 to 5 minutes per side or use your Air-Fryer at 375°F (190°C) for 16 to 18 minutes. Alternatively, bake in the oven at 350°F (180°C, or gas mark 4), on a baking sheet lined with parchment paper or a silicone baking mat, loosely covered in foil, for 15 minutes, and then flip and bake for 15 minutes longer, or until firm and warmed all the way through.

You Are SO Vegan!

Serve with slaw made with Dino Lacinato Kale instead of cabbage for an extra punch of green goodness!

ALL-THE-FIXIN'S HOLIDAY BURGER

No-Sugar Added   Nut Free

This here burger was the brainchild of my bestie, Jennifer. She said if I could pack an entire holiday dinner into a burger, she would be in heaven. So, I gave it a shot. I invited her over and had her test it out. She said it was like crack and . . . there you have it. I use boxed stuffing, but any bread-based stuffing will work fine. In fact, a few slices of stale bread, cut into cubes and mixed with butter and vegetable broth, then baked, makes a pretty darn good stuffing!

1 tablespoon (14 g) nondairy butter

1 cup (160 g) diced onion

2 tablespoons (30 g) minced garlic

4 cups (900 g) cooked mashed potatoes

4 cups (800 g) prepared bread stuffing

1 can (14 ounces [392 g]) cut green beans, drained

1 cup (96 g) Crispy Fried Onions, store-bought or homemade (page 222)

Salt and pepper

Oil, for frying (optional)

YIELD: 8 BURGERS

In a skillet over medium-high heat, melt the butter, add the onion and garlic, and sauté until just beginning to brown, 3 to 5 minutes.

Transfer to a bowl, add the potatoes, stuffing, green beans, fried onions, and salt and pepper to taste. Knead to combine.

Form into 8 patties. Cook as desired.

Panfry in oil for 3 to 5 minutes per side, or until crispy and golden; Air-Fry at 375°F (190°C) for 10 to 12 minutes; or bake at 350°F (180°C, or gas mark 4), on a baking sheet lined with parchment or a silicone baking mat, for about 20 minutes, flipping halfway through. Everything is already cooked—you just need to heat them up!

You Are SO Vegan!

Make this burger as an alternative to a huge elaborate holiday dinner or make it the day after out of the leftovers from the big meal.

MUSHROOM CHICKEN BURGER

No-Sugar Added *Gluten-Free* *Nut Free*

These are very neutral in flavor, so you can pretty much dress them up any way you want! I like them on a soft bun with mayo (page 197) and crispy iceburg lettuce.

1 cup (96 g) TVP granules

1 cup (235 ml) chicken-flavored vegetable broth

8 ounces (227 g) mushrooms, sliced or chopped to your desired size (I like mine chunky)

2 cloves garlic, minced

2 tablespoons (30 ml) olive oil

8 ounces (227 g) plain tempeh, crumbled into small bits

¼ cup (30 g) nutritional yeast

2 tablespoons (16 g) cornstarch

2½ tablespoons (19 g) ground flaxseed mixed with 3 tablespoons (45 ml) water

Salt and pepper

Oil, for frying (optional)

YIELD: 5 OR 6 BURGERS

In a microwave-safe bowl, mix together the TVP granules and the broth, cover tightly with plastic wrap, and microwave for 5 to 6 minutes. Alternatively, bring the broth to a boil, pour over the TVP granules, cover, and let sit for 10 minutes. Let cool.

In a pan, sauté the mushrooms and garlic in the oil for about 5 minutes, or until the mushrooms have reduced in size to about half. Lower the heat, add the crumbled tempeh, and cook for 5 minutes longer, being careful not to burn. Let cool.

In a mixing bowl, combine the TVP with the mushroom mixture, nutritional yeast, cornstarch, flax mixture, and salt and pepper to taste. Knead very well, using your hands, to get it all smooshed and mooshed together. Form into 5 or 6 patties and cook as desired.

I make these on the grill, individually wrapped loosely in foil, essentially steaming them. They stay very moist. They can also be panfried, microwaved, Air-Fried or baked. To bake them, bake at 350°F (180°C, or gas mark 4) for 15 minutes on each side, loosely covered with foil to prevent them from drying out, until firm and heated all the way through.

You Are SO Vegan!

Make your own "chicken" broth powder to keep on hand to add to veggie broth whenever you want a chicken-y flavor! Mix together 3 tablespoons (23 g) nutritional yeast with 1 tablespoon (2 g) dried parsley, 1 tablespoon (8 g) onion powder, 1 ½ teaspoons garlic powder, 1 teaspoon celery seed, ½ teaspoon salt, ½ teaspoon dried oregano, ½ teaspoon turmeric, ¼ teaspoon thyme, ¼ teaspoon dried rosemary, and ¼ teaspoon black pepper. Keep in an airtight container.

THE CRUNCH AND MUNCH BURGER

It's the crunch that keeps you coming back for more munch! The burger itself has so much crunch that it's best with a soft Sweet Potato Bun (page 211) and a dollop of vegan mayo (page 197).

2 tablespoons (30 ml) olive oil

8 ounces (227 g) mushrooms, sliced or chopped

3 cloves garlic, minced

¾ cup (180 ml) vegetable broth

1 cup (96 g) TVP granules

2 stalks celery, diced

¼ cup (27 g) shredded carrot

1 cup (70 g) shredded red or green cabbage

½ cup (65 g) whole cashews (raw or roasted is fine)

½ cup (72 g) vital wheat gluten flour, plus more if needed

¼ cup (60 g) nondairy sour cream, store-bought or homemade (page 198)

2 tablespoons (30 g) sweet pickle relish

1 tablespoon (8 g) ground mustard

1 tablespoon (8 g) onion powder

Salt and pepper

Oil, for frying

YIELD: 4 BURGERS

In a heavy-bottom skillet, heat the oil and sauté the mushrooms and garlic for 5 to 7 minutes, or until fragrant and beginning to brown.

Add the vegetable stock and bring to a simmer. Add the TVP granules, mix well, cover, and remove from the heat. Let sit for 10 minutes.

When cool enough to handle, add the celery, carrot, cabbage, cashews, flour, sour cream, relish, mustard, onion powder, and salt and pepper to taste, and mix well using your hands, adding more flour, a little bit at a time, if the dough is too sticky.

Place in the fridge to cool for about 20 minutes and help stiffen the dough.

Form into 4 patties.

These are best fried in a skillet with a little oil for 4 to 5 minutes per side, or until a nice crispy crust forms. Alternatively, use your Air-Fryer at 375°F (190°C) for 16 to 18 minutes, making sure to brush the patty with a smidge of oil first.

You Are SO Vegan!

Switch out the cabbage for sauerkraut and add 1 teaspoon dried dill to the mixture for an extra fermented pickly twist.

CURRIED CHICKPEA AND BROCCOLI BURGER

A chapter full of burgers inspired by the Middle East just wouldn't be complete without a recipe full of chickpeas and curry! This one tastes great even without a bun. A great way to serve it is in a pita or flatbread with Tangy Tahini Sauce (page 189). Serve alongside other Middle Eastern sides, such as dahl, saffron rice, or steamed veggies.

2 cans (15 ounces [425 g] each) chickpeas, drained and rinsed

1 tablespoon (15 g) minced garlic

2 tablespoons (32 g) tahini paste

1 tablespoon (15 ml) sesame oil

1 teaspoon green curry paste (you can use yellow curry powder for this as well, but it will be a bit milder)

½ cup (72 g) vital wheat gluten flour

Salt and pepper

1 cup (71 g) broccoli florets, steamed and chopped

Oil, for frying (optional)

YIELD: 6 TO 8 BURGERS

In a mixing bowl, combine the chickpeas, garlic, tahini, oil, curry paste, flour, and salt and pepper to taste.

Using your hands, mash everything together as if your life depended on it. (Alternatively, you can use a food processor to mix the ingredients together. Just pulse a few times so that everything is combined but still a little chunky.)

After you've mashed everything, add the broccoli and gently combine so it is evenly distributed. If your dough seems too wet, add a little more flour. If your dough seems too dry, add a little more sesame oil. Refrigerate for at least 20 minutes to thicken up a bit.

Form into 6 to 8 patties and cook as desired. These taste good baked *or* fried. If frying, sauté for 4 to 5 minutes per side, until golden and crispy. Alternatively, use your Air-Fryer at 375°F (190°C) for 14 to 16 minutes, brushing each side of the patties lightly with oil before placing them in the basket. If baking, use a baking sheet or baking pan, covering with a foil tent to keep in the moisture, and bake for 15 minutes at 350°F (180°C, or gas mark 4), then flip and bake 15 minutes longer, or until firm and just beginning to brown. Or you can bake them for 15 minutes, and then fry them . . . *mmmm.*

You Are SO Vegan!

For a gluten-free version, replace the vital wheat gluten with ¼ cup plus 2 tablespoons (45 g) besan (chickpea flour).

SUN-DRIED TOMATO AND ARTICHOKE BURGER

Gluten-Free

Nut Free

No-Sugar Added

Soy-Free

Feel free to cut this recipe in half. I just hate to use half of a can of anything, because I know I will forget to use the other half and it'll go bad. The patties freeze well, however, and reheat nicely for lunches. Serve on toasted gluten-free crusty bread or a roll with a schmear of Garlic Artichoke Spread (page 194).

2 tablespoons (30 ml) olive oil*

8 ounces (227 g) mushrooms, sliced

1 yellow onion, roughly chopped

2 tablespoons (30 g) minced garlic

Pinch of salt

1 can (14 ounces [392 g]) artichoke hearts, drained

¼ cup (28 g) sun-dried tomatoes, packed in oil

6 ounces (170 g) roasted red peppers, store-bought or homemade (see Fire Roasted Red Pepper Burger page 151)

¼ cup (30 g) nutritional yeast

2 cups (160 g) quick-cooking oats

3 cups (495 g) cooked brown rice**

Oil, for frying (optional)

*If trying to cut down on added fats, use nonstick cooking spray or a Misto filled with olive oil.

**I find that using vegetable broth instead of water when preparing the rice gives it a wonderful flavor.

___

YIELD: 8 TO 10 BURGERS

In a cast-iron skillet, heat the oil over medium-high heat and add the mushrooms, onion, garlic, and salt. Sauté for 5 to 7 minutes, or until very fragrant, translucent, and reduced by about half.

In a food processor, combine the artichokes, sun-dried tomatoes, peppers, nutritional yeast, oats, and rice. Add the sautéed mixture. Process until a uniform consistency is achieved. Transfer to a bowl and refrigerate for about 1 hour. This will allow the oats to absorb a lot of the moisture and make the patties easier to form.

Depending on the moisture content of your mix, you may want to add a little more or less oats.

Form into 8 to 10 patties and cook as desired. Panfry in oil over medium heat for 5 to 7 minutes per side, or until nice and crispy, Air-Fry at 375°F (190°C) for 16 to 18 minutes, or bake, loosely covered in a foil tent, at 350°F (180°C, or gas mark 4) for 15 minutes per side, or until firm and just beginning to brown.

You Are SO Vegan!

Skip the bun and serve with hummus and mixed greens. On the side? A nice green vegetable, such as broccoli, green beans, or asparagus.

TABBOULEH BURGER

No-Sugar Added · Nut Free · Soy-Free

Tabbouleh has a clean, light flavor that just tastes healthy. If you have a food processor, now is the time to use it.

FOR TABBOULEH SALAD:

3 cups (705 ml) water

1 cup (176 g) uncooked bulgur wheat

3 cups (180 g) finely chopped fresh parsley

1 large cucumber, seeded and diced (about 2 cups [270 g])

1 cup (180 g) diced tomatoes (approx. 2 seeded tomatoes)

¼ cup (12 g) finely chopped mint leaves

½ cup (120 ml) olive oil

3 tablespoons (45 g) minced garlic

3 tablespoons (45 ml) lemon juice

Salt and pepper

FOR BURGERS:

1 recipe Tabbouleh Salad (above)

1 cup (120 g) whole wheat flour

3 tablespoons (24 g) cornstarch

2 tablespoons (30 ml) sesame oil (optional)

YIELD: 10 BURGERS

To make the tabbouleh salad: Bring the water, lightly salted, to a boil. Add the bulgur wheat, lower the heat to a simmer, and cook, uncovered, for about 10 minutes, or until all the liquid is absorbed. Set aside to cool.

In a large bowl, combine the parsley, cucumber, tomatoes, mint, olive oil, garlic, lemon juice, and salt and pepper to taste. Add the cooled bulgur and mix thoroughly.

Stop here and you have a perfectly good tabbouleh salad. You don't have to make it into burgers.

To make the burgers: Preheat the oven to 350°F (180°C, or gas mark 4). Line a baking pan with parchment or a silicone baking mat.

Add the flour and cornstarch to the Tabbouleh Salad mixture. Knead until well incorporated. If your mixture is too wet, add a little more flour. Form into 10 patties. Bake for 40 to 45 minutes, flipping halfway through, until firm and just beginning to brown. You can eat them just like this, but they get extra yummy if you panfry them in a little sesame oil after you bake them, just to get a little golden crispy crust! Alternatively, use your Air-Fryer at 375°F (190°C) for 18 to 20 minutes.

You Are SO Vegan!

Vegans LOVE potlucks, and because these taste great warm or cold, make these into little slider appetizers to bring along to the next vegan potluck in your neck of the woods. Make 20 burger patties instead of 10 as listed above and reduce the cook time by 10 minutes (3 to 4 minutes less in the Air-Fryer). Start with slider-size 50/50 flatbreads (page 207). Add a bit of hummus, a few leaves of baby spinach, a slice of Roma tomato, and a dollop of Tzatziki Sauce (page 199).

ZUCCHINI MUSHROOM BURGER

No-Sugar Added

Nut Free

These burgers are nice and juicy and full of flavor, just as a burger should be. I serve this on a hearty wheat bun topped with Chunky Marinara (page 194). With all of the amazing vegan cheeses out there these days, a nice pile of melted vegan Mozzarella would be super tasty on this guy.

2 tablespoons (30 ml) olive oil, plus more for frying (optional)

8 ounces (227 g) mushrooms (I used white buttons, but portobellos would be yummy here, too), chopped or sliced

1 yellow or white onion, chopped

2 tablespoons (30 g) minced garlic

1 cup (235 ml) vegetable broth

1 cup (96 g) TVP granules

1 cup (124 g) grated or shredded zucchini

2½ tablespoons (19 g) ground flax-seed mixed with 3 tablespoons (45 ml) warm water

1 cup (144 g) vital wheat gluten flour

Salt and pepper

YIELD: 8 BURGERS

Heat the 2 tablespoons (30 ml) olive oil in a pan and sauté the mushrooms, onion, and garlic until reduced by half, slightly browned, and fragrant, 7 to 10 minutes. Add the vegetable broth and bring to a simmer. Add the TVP granules, stir to combine, cover, and remove from the heat. Let sit for 10 minutes.

Transfer to a mixing bowl and add the zucchini, flax mixture, flour, and salt and pepper to taste. Knead with your hands until very well incorporated. Depending on the amount of moisture in your vegetables, you may need to add a little extra flour. Cover and refrigerate for at least 20 minutes to thicken up a bit. Form into 8 patties and cook as desired.

If frying, use a heavy-bottom skillet with plenty of oil and fry for 3 to 4 minutes per side, or until golden and crispy. Alternatively, use your Air-Fryer at 375°F (190°C) for 16 to 18 minutes. If baking, use a baking sheet lined with parchment or a silicone baking mat, and bake, covered in a foil tent, at 350°F (180°C, or gas mark 4) for 15 to 20 minutes per side, until firm and just beginning to brown.

You Are SO Vegan!

Don't have access to vegan cheese at your local market? Make some cheesy sauce to drizzle over the top from scratch! Follow the recipe for the Nacho Cheesy Sauce (page 188) but replace the cumin, jalapeños, and jalapeño juice with the same amounts of basil, chopped sun-dried tomatoes packed in oil, and the oil from the tomatoes. It makes a lovely topping for this burger, as well as for steamed veggies. Especially broccoli!

SUMMER SQUASH BURGER

No-Sugar Added

Nut Free

These patties make a great breakfast, lunch, or dinner, depending on how you serve them. For breakfast, serve this bunless alongside a tofu scramble. For lunch, serve this patty on whole wheat toast with a schmear of vegan mayo (page 197) and avocado. For dinner, serve on a crusty bun with a side of beans or potato salad.

1 cup (124 g) shredded yellow zucchini

1 cup (124 g) shredded green zucchini

2 cups (250 g) all-purpose flour

6 ounces (170 g) plain soy or other nondairy yogurt

¼ cup (60 ml) mild flavored vegetable oil, plus more for frying

¼ cup (60 ml) soy or other nondairy milk

¼ teaspoon paprika

Salt and pepper

YIELD: 4 BURGERS

In a mixing bowl, combine the zucchinis, flour, yogurt, ¼ cup (60 ml) oil, milk, paprika, and salt and pepper to taste, mashing it together with your hands until you get a nice uniform mixture.

Form into 4 patties. Line a plate with paper towels.

Preheat ¼ inch (6 mm) oil in a frying pan over medium-high heat. The oil is ready when a piece of dough dropped into it sizzles immediately. Carefully add the patties, and fry for 3 to 4 minutes per side, until golden and crispy. Transfer to the plate to absorb the excess oil.

You Are SO Vegan!

Instead of making burgers, try making mini versions of these and serving them like fritters as a side dish alongside your favorite protein.

Chapter 8

SEITAN-BASED BURGERS

Gluten-full and proud of it!

SEITANIC STUFFER

Nut Free

No-Sugar Added

This is really four separate burgers! Yummy, "beefy" outer burgers with yummy, gooey surprises inside. Actually, you could probably make 101 versions of just this burger. Once you make the burger dough, you can pretty much stuff them with anything you want (the four Stuffer recipes that follow are my favorites). No matter which stuffer you make, know that these fellas are whoppers (no pun intended), so make sure to keep the sides light and green if possible.

FOR BURGER DOUGH:

2 cups (288 g) vital wheat gluten flour

1 cup (120 g) whole wheat flour

¼ cup (30 g) nutritional yeast

2 tablespoons (16 g) garlic powder

2 tablespoons (16 g) onion powder

2 tablespoons (4 g) dried parsley

1 teaspoon paprika

Salt and pepper (I like a lot of black pepper in mine!)

1 cup (235 ml) vegetable broth

⅔ cup (160 ml) Bragg's Liquid Aminos or soy sauce (if using regular soy sauce, use ⅓ cup [80 ml] soy sauce plus ⅓ cup [80 ml] water or vegetable broth)

⅓ cup (80 ml) olive oil

¼ cup (66 g) tomato paste

FOR FILLING:

Filling of your choice (pages 115–119)

YIELD: 6 BURGERS

Preheat the oven to 350°F (180°C, or gas mark 4). Line a baking sheet with parchment or a silicone baking mat.

In a large mixing bowl, combine the flours, nutritional yeast, garlic powder, onion powder, parsley, paprika, and salt and pepper to taste.

In a separate bowl, combine the broth, liquid aminos, oil, and tomato paste. Add the wet ingredients to the dry and knead vigorously for about 5 minutes. Let rest for about 20 minutes.

Form the dough into 12 patties and place on the prepared baking sheet. Scoop a good amount, about ¼ cup (65 g), of filling into the center of 6 of the patties. Sandwich the other 6 patties on top and pinch together the edges. Cover the baking sheet with foil to prevent them from drying out.

Bake for approximately 60 minutes, until firm, flipping half way through.

You Are SO Vegan!

I love old-school seitan recipes. I also love that seitan has ben having a bit of a resurgence of late. There is even an amazing Facebook group called the *Seitan Appreciation Society*. If you love seitan, too, and are looking for some incredible inspiration and recipes, I highly suggest you join up!

INSIDE-OUT CHEESEBURGER SEITANIC STUFFER

No-Sugar Added

This is the recipe for "Nutty Cheeze" from my first book, Cozy Inside. This recipe makes way more than you will need to stuff the burgers, but who doesn't need some extra yummy, sliceable cheeze in the fridge? Dress this as you would any cheeseburger. This one tastes especially great on thick slices of grilled sour dough. Serve up with a nice, crisp garden salad.

1 ounce (28 g) agar flakes or powder

3 cups (705 ml) water

2 cups (260 g) raw cashews, finely ground into a powder

3 tablespoons (45 ml) fresh lemon juice

2 tablespoons (30 ml) sesame oil

¼ cup (30 g) nutritional yeast

2 teaspoons (11 g) sea salt

½ teaspoon onion powder

½ teaspoon garlic powder

1 recipe Seitanic Stuffer (opposite page)

Spray a loaf pan with nonstick spray and set aside.

In a stockpot, combine the agar and the water and bring to a full boil; boil for 5 minutes. Whisk regularly.

In a food processor, combine the cashew powder, lemon juice, sesame oil, nutritional yeast, salt, onion powder, and garlic powder, and blend until well incorporated.

Pour into the water-agar mixture and mix until creamy and smooth; remove from the heat.

Pour into the prepared loaf pan and refrigerate for at least 1 hour, or until hardened.

Use as a filling for the Seitanic Stuffer dough (opposite page).

You Are SO Vegan!

You can make several variations by adding fresh herbs and spices to the mix. When I want a Mediterranean cheese, I add sun-dried tomatoes and fresh basil. When I want a Mexican cheese, I add cumin and chopped jalapeños. If I want a smoky cheese, I add a little bit of liquid smoke. It's limitless! I really like to use this recipe for the Double Down (page 162) and make it into nutty pepper jack by adding ¼ cup (25 g) jarred sliced jalapeños, diced, and ¼ cup (25 g) diced pimiento peppers to the mix.

GARLIC, MUSHROOM, AND ONION SEITANIC STUFFER

Nut Free

No-Sugar Added

I love this classic combo of ingredients. Serve on a toasted onion bun spread with Simple Pesto (page 193) and topped with fresh, juicy slices of yellow or red tomatoes. Let the burger be the star and keep the sides simple—and what could be simpler than a handful of chips?

1 cup (160 g) diced onion

8 ounces (227 g) mushrooms, sliced

2 tablespoons (30 g) minced garlic

2 tablespoons (30 ml) olive oil

½ cup (120 ml) vegetable broth

¼ cup (60 ml) soy sauce

2 tablespoons (16 g) all-purpose flour

1 recipe Seitanic Stuffer (page 114)

In a skillet or frying pan, sauté the onion, mushrooms, and garlic in the oil over medium-high heat until the mushrooms have reduced in volume by about half, 5 to 7 minutes.

Add the vegetable broth and soy sauce and bring to a simmer. Reduce the heat to low.

Sprinkle in the flour and stir until thickened. Use as a filling for the Seitanic Stuffer dough (page 114).

You Are SO Vegan!

Not only does this filling work smashingly for the Seitanic Stuffer, but it also works well in phyllo triangles, samosas, and puff pastry.

SPANAKOPITA-ISH SEITANIC STUFFER

This makes more filling than you will need for the burgers, so feel free to cut the recipe in half. Or make the whole thing and use the leftovers inside phyllo triangles or inside a tortilla for a quick and easy wrap for lunch.

14 ounces (396 g) extra-firm tofu, drained, pressed, and crumbled

1 can (14 ounces [392 g]) spinach, drained, or 2 cups (60 g) fresh spinach leaves, cut into chiffonade

½ cup (80 g) finely diced white or yellow onion

⅓ cup (40 g) pine nuts

⅓ cup (37 g) finely chopped sun-dried tomatoes

¼ cup (30 g) nutritional yeast

2 tablespoons (16 g) garlic powder

1 tablespoon (15 ml) lemon juice

Salt and pepper

1 recipe Seitanic Stuffer (page 114)

In a bowl, combine all the ingredients. Mix until well incorporated. Using your hands yields the best results. Refrigerate until ready to use. Use as a filling for the Seitanic Stuffer dough (page 114).

You Are SO Vegan!

Keep the Greek theme going by spreading a little hummus on a toasty bun before serving. Top the whole thing off with a few Kalamata olives skewered on a toothpick.

SMOKY TEMPEH SEITANIC STUFFER

No-Sugar Added

Nut Free

Oh! The smoky tender juiciness of this filling is the perfect way to introduce tempeh to those who might be just a little bit tempeh-timid. Serve this savory burger on a hearty bun with minimal dressing . . . maybe a bit of vegan mayo (page 197).

8 ounces (227 g) plain soy tempeh, crumbled

1 cup (160 g) finely diced onion

¼ cup (30 g) nutritional yeast

3 tablespoons (54 g) white or yellow miso

3 tablespoons (18 g) imitation bacon bits, store-bought or homemade (page 201)

1 tablespoon (7 g) paprika

¼ teaspoon liquid smoke

Black pepper

1 recipe Seitanic Stuffer (page 114)

Mix all the ingredients together until fully incorporated. Use as a filling for the Seitanic Stuffer dough (page 114).

You Are SO Vegan!

Serve alongside a big pile of steamed or sautéed greens such as kale or collards to round out the meal.

JAMAICAN JERK BURGER

Nut Free   No-Sugar Added

No-Oil Added

Spicy, spicy, spicy! Yet, strangely sweet! Traditional jerk uses Scotch bonnet chiles. These are a bit hard to find, and extremely hot! If you cannot find, or do not want to find, Scotch bonnets, you can reduce the heat a tad by using habaneros or jalapeños. But, even with jalapeños, these will be spicy. The jerk sauce can also be used to rub onto tofu or tempeh before baking or grilling.

FOR JERK SAUCE:

2 bunches (5 ounces [140 g]) green onions, whites and light green parts only

¼ cup (32 g) ground allspice

¼ cup (60 ml) pineapple juice (from the can, see below)

8 cloves garlic

6 to 8 Scotch bonnet chiles, seeded and cored

1 tablespoon (8 g) ground thyme

1 teaspoon ground cinnamon

½ teaspoon ground nutmeg

½ teaspoon sea salt

½ teaspoon freshly ground black pepper

FOR BURGERS:

24 ounces (680 g) prepared seitan, store-bought or homemade (page 203), roughly chopped

1 white onion, roughly chopped

1 recipe Jerk Sauce (above)

8 pineapple rings, reserving the juice from the can

YIELD: 2 CUPS (470 ML) SAUCE, 8 BURGERS

To make the jerk sauce: Place all the ingredients in a food processor and process until a paste forms. Transfer to a large bowl.

To make the burgers: Preheat the oven to 350°F (180°C, or gas mark 4). Line a baking sheet with parchment or a silicone baking mat.

In a food processor, combine the seitan and onion and process until crumbly.

Add to the Jerk Sauce and knead to combine.

Form into 8 patties and place on the prepared baking sheet. Place a pineapple ring on top of each patty before baking.

Bake, uncovered, for 45 minutes, until firm and browned.

You Are SO Vegan!

Serve on a soft white bun with a schmear of vegan mayo (page 197), topped with a grilled pineapple (or baked with the pineapple on top) and some pineapple orange pomegranate relish. Make the relish by adding 1 cup (235 ml) pineapple juice, ½ cup (120 ml) orange juice, ¼ cup (60 ml) olive oil, and 1 cup (181 g) crushed pineapple to a boil. Lower the heat to a simmer and simmer for 20 minutes. Remove from heat and stir in 1 cup (135 g) pomegranate seeds, ½ cup (50 g) chopped green onions, and salt and pepper to taste. Refrigerate until ready to use.

ORTEGA BURGER

Nut Free

No-Oil Added

These only take about 10 minutes to make, are loaded with protein, are super low in fat and carbs, but are super high in flavor! Garnish with grilled Ortega chiles, onions, jalapeño, nondairy sour cream, salsa, and avocado. Serve with tortilla chips, guacamole, and salsa on the side.

---

1 cup (96 g) TVP granules

1 scant cup (225 ml) water

2 tablespoons (16 g) taco seasoning, store-bought or homemade (page 201)

½ cup (72 g) vital wheat gluten flour

½ cup (80 g) your favorite salsa*

1 tablespoon (15 ml) hot sauce

*If your salsa is really juicy, you might have to add a little extra flour.

YIELD: 4 BURGERS

In a microwave-safe bowl, mix together the TVP granules and the water, cover tightly with plastic wrap, and microwave for 5 to 6 minutes. Alternatively, bring the water to a boil, pour over the TVP granules, cover, and let sit for 10 minutes. Let cool.

Mix in the taco seasoning, then mix in the flour, salsa, and hot sauce. Let sit for about 20 minutes or refrigerate until ready to serve.

Form into 4 patties. Cook as desired.

These can be baked at 350°F (180°C, or gas mark 4), uncovered, for about 15 minutes per side, or until just crisp on the outside; Air-Fried at 375°F (190°C) for 12 to 14 minutes; or grilled. If grilling, wrap in foil so they don't fall apart. If you aren't worried about added oil, they can be panfried in a smidge of oil or nonstick spray, for 3 to 5 minutes per side, until golden and crispy.

You Are SO Vegan!

These burgers taste great crumbled up as a topping for a Mexican inspired bowl. Start with a base of Cilantro Lime Rice (page 227) and use the same garnishes listed above.

SPLIT PEAS WITH HAMBURGER

Nut Free

Soy-Free

It's like cramming a big bowl of split pea soup with chunks of ham into a burger!
Serve this on a nice crusty piece of toasted sourdough or French bread.

FOR "HAM":

½ cup (60 g) chickpea flour

½ cup (72 g) vital wheat gluten flour

½ cup (120 ml) water or vegetable broth

¼ cup (60 ml) mild-flavored vegetable oil

2 tablespoons (28 g) brown sugar

2 tablespoons (15 g) nutritional yeast

1½ tablespoons (25 g) tomato paste

½ teaspoon liquid smoke

½ teaspoon black pepper

¼ teaspoon salt

FOR BURGERS:

4 cups (940 ml) vegetable broth

2 cups (450 g) dried split peas

½ cup (62 g) all-purpose flour

½ cup (120 ml) canola oil, plus more for frying

2 tablespoons (16 g) onion powder

Salt and pepper

YIELD: 8 BURGERS

To make the "ham": Preheat the oven to 350°F (180°C, or gas mark 4).

In a mixing bowl, mix together all the "ham" ingredients until a nice goopy mixture forms. Spread a large sheet of aluminum foil on the counter. Plop the mixture into the middle of the foil. Roll the foil over the mixture, and twist the ends tight, so that a nice log is formed. Place on a baking sheet, seam side down, and bake for about 45 minutes, or until firm. Remove from the oven and let cool.

Slice off a piece for yourself to snack on while you are cooking the split peas. Chop up the remaining "ham" into ½-inch (1.3 cm) cubes for the burgers.

To make the burgers: In a pot, combine the broth and split peas. Cover and bring to a boil. Lower the heat to a simmer, and cook for 15 minutes longer. Remove the lid, and continue cooking until tender and most of the liquid is absorbed, 5 to 7 minutes longer.

Transfer 3 cups (596 g) prepared peas to a mixing bowl and let cool. Add the chopped "ham", flour, the ½ cup (120 ml) oil, onion powder, and salt and pepper to taste, and knead with your hands. Form into 8 patties. Panfry in oil over medium-high heat for 3 to 5 minutes per side. Alternatively, use your Air-Fryer at 375°F (190°C) for 16 to 18 minutes. Although these taste best fried, they can also be baked at 350°F (180°C, or gas mark 4) for 15 minutes per side, loosely covered in foil, until firm and warmed all the way through.

You Are SO Vegan!

Use the ham recipe above to make the Midwest classic dish ... *Ham Salad!* Cubed and cooled ham is mixed with vegan mayo, chopped celery, pickle relish, and shredded carrots.

PEPPERONI PIZZA BURGER

Pepperoni pizza as a burger? Whhaaaat? For extra pizza goodness, place some shredded vegan mozzarella on the top of your burger during the last few minutes of cooking to get it all nice and melty. For a bun? Try garlic naan or 50/50 Flatbread (page 207, and pictured here), schmeared with Simple Pesto (page 195, and pictured here).

1 tablespoon (8 g) freshly ground black pepper

1 tablespoon (7 g) paprika

1 teaspoon whole aniseed

1 teaspoon salt

1 teaspoon red pepper flakes

1 teaspoon sugar

1 teaspoon dried basil

1 teaspoon chipotle powder or cayenne pepper

1 tablespoon (8 g) garlic powder

1 cup (96 g) TVP granules

1 cup (235 ml) water

2 tablespoons (30 ml) liquid smoke

2 tablespoons (30 ml), plus ¼ cup (60 ml) olive oil, divided

6 ounces (170 g) tomato paste

1 cup (144 g) vital wheat gluten flour

⅓ cup (80 g) nondairy sour cream, store-bought or homemade (page 198)

Oil, for frying (optional)

YIELD: 6 BURGERS

In a microwave-safe dish, combine the pepper, paprika, aniseed, salt, red pepper flakes, sugar, basil, chipotle powder, garlic powder, TVP, water, liquid smoke, and 2 tablespoons (30 ml) olive oil. Cover tightly with plastic wrap and microwave on high for 5 to 6 minutes. Alternatively, bring the water to a boil and pour over the TVP mixed with the spices, oil, and liquid smoke, cover, and let sit for 10 minutes. Let cool.

Add the tomato paste, flour, remaining ¼ cup (60 g) oil, and sour cream to the cooled TVP mixture. Using your hands, mash everything together and form into 6 patties.

You can panfry, Air-Fry, or bake these with great results. Panfry in just a smidge of oil for 5 minutes per side over medium-high heat, or until a nice crispy crust forms. Air-Fry at 375°F (190°C) for 16 to 18 minutes. Or bake them at 350°F (180°C, or gas mark 4) on a baking sheet lined with parchment or a silicone baking mat, uncovered, for 30 minutes, flipping halfway through.

You Are SO Vegan!

Make the ultimate pizza pockets using premade pizza dough! Preheat your oven to 425°F (220°C, or gas mark 7). Line a baking sheet with parchment. Divide dough into 6 pieces, and roll out thin on a well-floured surface. Place a dollop of Chunky Marinara (page 194) or Simple Pesto (page 193) on one half of the dough, add Pepperoni Pizza Burger on top of sauce, and place a handful of vegan mozzarella shreds on top. Fold other half of the dough over and seal edges with tines of a fork. Slice 2 to 3 vent holes in top with a sharp knife. Brush lightly with melted vegan butter. Sprinkle with a pinch of dried basil and paprika. Bake 12 to 15 minutes, or until crust is golden.

JALAPEÑO CHEDDAR BURGER

Not too spicy, but just enough kick to know it's there. The cheddar flavor comes from the miso and nutritional yeast. Serve on a toasted bun with a healthy dollop of Sweet Mustard Sauce (page 198) and a side of Cilantro Lime Rice (page 227).

1 cup (96 g) **TVP granules**

1 cup (235 ml) **vegetable broth**

¼ cup (30 g) **nutritional yeast**

1 teaspoon **liquid smoke**

12 slices **jarred jalapeños**, or to taste, diced

2 cloves **garlic**, minced

2 tablespoons (36 g) **white or yellow miso**

¼ cup (60 g) **nondairy cream cheese**

1 cup (144 g) **vital wheat gluten flour**

Oil, for frying (optional)

————————

YIELD: 4 BURGERS

In a microwave-safe dish, combine the TVP, vegetable broth, nutritional yeast, and liquid smoke. Cover tightly with plastic wrap and microwave for 5 to 6 minutes. Alternatively, bring the water to a boil, pour over the TVP granules, nutritional yeast, and liquid smoke, cover, and let sit for 10 minutes. Let cool.

Add the jalapeños, garlic, miso, cream cheese, and flour to the TVP mixture and knead together until a thick, well-blended dough is formed. Allow to rest for 20 minutes. Form into 4 patties and cook as desired.

These taste great both fried and baked. They are also sturdy enough to grill, so have at it!

Panfry in oil over medium heat for 3 to 4 minutes per side, or until golden and crispy; Air-Fry at 375°F (190°C) for 14 to 16 minutes. Or, bake at 350°F (180°C, or gas mark 4), uncovered, on a baking sheet lined with parchment or a silicone baking mat, for 25 minutes, flipping halfway through.

To grill, find a spot on the grill over a medium-low flame, and cook for 5 to 7 minutes per side, remembering to add a little oil to the patties before placing them on the grill to ensure those pretty grill marks!

You Are SO Vegan!

Top with roasted jalapeños to take it up a notch. Wrap a few whole fresh jalapeños in a foil pouch and throw them on the grill for about 30 minutes. Allow to cool enough to handle and cut off the stem. Slice lengthwise and scrape out the seeds.

SWEET AND SOUR PORK MINI BURGER

Nut Free

The sauce here also tastes great tossed with your favorite veggie protein and served over rice and steamed veggies. Serve on a Soft White Bun (page 206) with crunchy shredded cabbage. Add a side of stir-fried veggies and sticky rice to round out the meal.

FOR SAUCE:

¾ cup (180 ml) pineapple juice

¼ cup (50 g) sugar

2 tablespoons (34 g) ketchup

2 tablespoons (30 ml) soy sauce

1 teaspoon red pepper flakes

¼ cup (60 ml) rice wine vinegar

1 tablespoon (8 g) cornstarch dissolved in ¼ cup (60 ml) water to make a slurry

FOR BURGERS:

Oil, for frying

½ cup (120 ml) soymilk

½ cup (62 g) all-purpose flour

¼ cup (32 g) cornstarch

1 recipe "Ham" (page 123)

YIELD: 12 MINI BURGERS

To make the sauce: In a saucepan, combine the pineapple juice, sugar, ketchup, soy sauce, and red pepper flakes. Bring to a boil. Stir in the vinegar. Turn off the heat and stir in the cornstarch slurry. Stir until thickened. Keep warm over very low heat until the burgers are ready to coat.

To make the burgers: Preheat ¼ inch (6 mm) of oil in a frying pan over high heat. The oil is ready when a piece of dough dropped into it sizzles immediately.

Pour the soymilk into a shallow dish. In another shallow dish, combine the flour and cornstarch.

Slice the "ham" into 12 slices, each ¼-inch (6 mm)-thick. Dip each slice into the soymilk, and then dredge in the flour mixture.

Fry for 2 to 3 minutes per side, or until crispy and golden brown.

Transfer directly to the sauce and turn to coat.

You Are SO Vegan!

Instead of making burgers, make skewers of sweet and sour pork, bell peppers, and pineapple. Follow the recipe above, but cut the ham into cubes instead of slices.

OKTOBERFEST KRAUT BURGER

Nut Free No-Oil Added No-Sugar Added Soy-Free

No vegan beer garden in your town? No biggie. Make your own kraut burgers to snack on between those pints of brew. Speaking of kraut, choose yours wisely. True sauerkraut is fermented, not pickled in vinegar. Check ingredient labels and choose one that only contains cabbage, salt, and spices.

2 cups (288 g) vital wheat gluten flour

¼ cup (30 g) nutritional yeast

1 tablespoon (8 g) garlic powder

1 tablespoon (8 g) onion powder

1 tablespoon (2 g) dried parsley

1 teaspoon freshly ground black pepper

1½ cups (355 ml) vegetable broth

½ cup (120 g) sauerkraut, drained

YIELD: 8 BURGERS

Preheat the oven to 350°F (180°C, or gas mark 4). Line a baking sheet with parchment or a silicone baking mat.

In a mixing bowl, combine the flour, nutritional yeast, garlic powder, onion powder, parsley, and black pepper. Slowly add the vegetable broth and stir to combine.

Add the sauerkraut and knead until uniform and consistent. Cover and let sit for about 20 minutes to allow the gluten to rest.

Form into 8 patties and place on the prepared baking sheet. Cover the entire pan loosely with foil.

Bake for 20 minutes, then flip and bake for 20 minutes longer, until firm and warmed all the way through.

You Are SO Vegan!

Serve up with lots of extra kraut, grilled onions, and spicy brown mustard on a soft white bun. Making a full-on meal? Add a side of roasted Brussels sprouts to your plate for extra vegan points.

CHICKEN FRIED STEAK BURGER

Greasy breakfasts are my number one way to cure an aching belly after a night of too much fun. They're also one of my favorite ways to make dinner! Serve open-faced on Cheesy Biscuits (page 208) topped with your favorite gravy.

FOR THE PATTIES:

1 pound (454 g) prepared seitan, store-bought or homemade (page 203)

½ cup (62 g) all-purpose flour

¼ cup (60 ml) vegetable oil

1 tablespoon (2 g) dried parsley or 3 tablespoons (12 g) chopped fresh parsley

Salt and pepper

Oil, for frying

FOR THE BREADING:

1 cup (125 g) all-purpose flour

¼ cup (30 g) nutritional yeast

1 teaspoon paprika

Salt and pepper

1 cup (235 ml) nondairy milk

YIELD: 4 BURGERS

To make the patties: Combine all the ingredients in a food processor and process until a dough ball forms. If your mixture is too dry, add in a little more oil, 1 teaspoon (5 ml) at a time. If it is too wet, add in a little more flour, 1 tablespoon (8 g) at a time.

Divide the dough into 4 equal pieces and form into patties. Set aside.

To make the breading: Mix together all the ingredients except milk and place in a shallow dish. Place the milk in a separate shallow dish.

Dip each patty into the milk, then dredge in the flour mixture, then dip into the milk again, and then dredge in the flour mixture again. This is known as *double dredging*.

Preheat a skillet with plenty of oil. Fry each patty for approximately 5 minutes per side, or until very golden brown and crispy.

You Are SO Vegan!

To make a simple white gravy, to a sauce pot, melt ¼ cup (56 g) vegan butter over medium-high heat. Stir in ¼ cup (31 g) all-purpose flour and cook until golden. Add in 2 cups (470 ml) water or broth, and cook until thickened, stir in lots of black pepper and salt taste.

ETHIOPIAN BERBERE BURGER

Nut Free

No-Sugar Added

The exotic spices and aromas here really take this burger to a whole new level. These are a bit labor-intensive, but wow, they are so worth it.

FOR BERBERE SPICE MIXTURE:

2 teaspoons (4 g) whole cumin seeds

4 whole cloves

½ teaspoon black peppercorns

¼ teaspoon whole allspice

1 dried ancho chile, with seeds, ground into a powder

3 tablespoons (21 g) smoked paprika

1 teaspoon ground ginger

¼ teaspoon turmeric

¼ teaspoon ground cinnamon

1 teaspoon salt

FOR BURGERS:

1 cup (144 g) vital wheat gluten flour

2 cups (240 g) whole wheat flour

1 recipe Berbere Spice Mixture (above)

¼ cup (60 ml) olive oil

2 cups (470 ml) water

4 cups (940 ml) vegetable broth

2 tablespoons (16 g) all-purpose flour dissolved in ¼ cup (60 ml) water to make a slurry

---

YIELD: 6 TO 8 BURGERS

To make the spice mixture: In a dry pan, toast the cumin seeds, cloves, peppercorns, and allspice for 1 to 2 minutes. Take care not to burn.

Grind the whole spices into a powder and add the chile powder, paprika, ginger, turmeric, cinnamon, and salt. Mix well.

To make the burgers: In a large mixing bowl, combine the flours and berbere spice mixture. Add the oil and water and knead for 5 straight minutes. Cover lightly with a dish towel and let sit for at least 30 minutes. Form into 6 to 8 patties.

Bring the vegetable broth to a boil in a wide shallow pan (a cast-iron skillet works nicely here). Add the patties to the boiling broth in a single layer, being careful not to crowd the pan. You may have to do these in 2 batches.

Lower the heat to a simmer, cover, and simmer for 1 hour, checking to make sure the patties are not stuck to the bottom of the pan.

Remove the patties from the broth with a slotted spoon. Slowly add the flour slurry to the broth remaining in the pan and stir until thickened.

Serve the gravy in a dish for dipping.

You Are SO Vegan!

Do yourself a favor and find some authentic injera to serve with this. The texture and flavor are so nice, and it really does a good job of soaking up that gravy!

BROOSKETTA BURGER

I so enjoy the bruschetta topping on this burger that I often make it to mix with pasta or simply serve over crostini. Serve on a toasted piece of Italian bread, or better yet, garlic bread, piled high with a generous helping of bruschetta topping, as shown here.

FOR BRUSCHETTA TOPPING:

12 ounces (340 g) extra-firm tofu, drained and pressed

20 leaves fresh basil, cut into chiffonade

2 tablespoons (30 g) minced garlic

¼ cup (60 ml) olive oil

1 cup (180 g) diced Roma tomatoes, seeded

Salt and pepper, to taste

FOR BURGERS:

1 cup (96 g) TVP granules

1 cup (235 ml) vegetable broth

½ cup (72 g) vital wheat gluten flour

½ cup plus 2 tablespoons (6 ounces, or 170 g) tomato paste

¼ cup (30 g) nutritional yeast

1 cup (259 g) Bruschetta Topping (above), plus extra for serving

Salt and pepper

YIELD: 6 BURGERS

To make the topping: Chop the tofu into tiny, tiny cubes, about ⅛ inch (3 mm), if possible. Mix together all the ingredients and let sit for a few hours to really let the flavors meld.

To make the burgers: Preheat the oven to 350°F (180°C, or gas mark 4). Line a baking sheet with parchment or a silicone baking mat.

In a microwave-safe bowl, mix together the TVP granules and the broth, cover tightly with plastic wrap, and microwave for 5 to 6 minutes. Alternatively, bring the broth to a boil, pour over the TVP, cover, and let sit for 10 minutes.

Combine the reconstituted TVP, flour, tomato paste, nutritional yeast, bruschetta topping, and salt and pepper. Use your hands to really mush it all together. Form into 6 patties and place on the prepared baking sheet.

Bake, uncovered, for 15 minutes, then flip and bake for 15 minutes longer.

Top with a pile of extra bruschetta.

You Are SO Vegan!

Make these into appetizers by making mini burgers and serving open faced on toasted crostini. Drizzle with a balsamic reduction to be extra fancy.

BURGER ROLL-UPS

No-Sugar Added

Otherwise known as a roulade, this recipe is sliced and eaten as burgers. One roll yields 10 to 12 burgers, so there's plenty left over for work lunches and quick weeknight heat-ups. Serve on a Sweet Potato Bun (page 211) with vegan mayo (page 197).

FOR SEITAN DOUGH:

2 cups (288 g) vital wheat gluten flour

1 cup (120 g) whole wheat flour

½ cup (60 g) nutritional yeast

2 tablespoons (16 g) vegetable broth powder

2 tablespoons (16 g) garlic powder

2 tablespoons (16 g) onion powder

½ teaspoon paprika

Salt and pepper, to taste

2 cups (470 ml) water

½ cup (120 ml) olive oil

FOR FILLING:

8 ounces (227 g) extra-firm tofu, drained, pressed, and crumbled

3 tablespoons (45 g) nondairy cream cheese

2 tablespoons (16 g) ground raw cashews

2 tablespoons (15 g) pine nuts

1 cup (180 g) diced tomatoes, drained

1 cup (227 g) canned or frozen spin-ach, drained

½ cup (80 g) diced onion

2 tablespoons (15 g) nutritional yeast

1 tablespoon (15 g) minced garlic

YIELD: 10 TO 12 BURGERS

To make the seitan dough: In a mixing bowl, combine the flours, nutritional yeast, vegetable broth powder, garlic powder, onion powder, paprika, and salt and pepper, to taste. Add water and oil and knead for about 5 minutes. Cover and let sit for 20 minutes.

Preheat the oven to 350°F (180°C, or gas mark 4). Line a baking sheet with parchment or a silicone baking mat.

To make the filling: Mush all the filling ingredients together in a bowl and set aside until ready to use.

Next, roll out the dough into a large rectangle. Transfer to the prepared baking sheet and bake, uncovered, for 20 minutes.

Remove from the oven (do not turn off the oven) and spread on the filling to about 1 inch (2.5 cm) from the edges. Roll up tightly and place seam side down on a large sheet of aluminum foil, roll up, and twist the edges tight. Place on the baking sheet and bake for 60 to 70 minutes, until firm. Remove from the oven and let sit until cool enough to handle.

Unwrap and cut into 10 to 12 slices, ½ to ¾ inch (1.3 to 1.9 cm) thick, and serve on your favorite bun.

You Are SO Vegan!

Don't be limited by this recipe for filling. You can fill your Burger Roll-Ups with a multitude of fillings. How about Bacon Cheeseburger Roll-Ups? What about Car-melized Onion and Fig Burger Roll-Ups? Get creative!

Chapter 9

GLUTEN-FREE BURGERS

No wheat? No Problem!

SUN-DRIED TOMATO AND PESTO BURGER

Gluten-Free *No-Sugar Added* *Soy-Free*

This one is good on two crusty pieces of bread, grilled like a panini, schmeared with extra pesto and a few fresh leaves of spinach.

1 tablespoon (15 ml) olive oil, plus more for frying (optional)

8 ounces (227 g) mushrooms, sliced or chopped

1 white or yellow onion, chopped

¼ cup (28 g) sun-dried tomato pieces, packed in oil, drained

2 cups (330 g) cooked brown rice

1 recipe Simple Pesto (page 193)

Salt and pepper

½ to 1 cup (80 to 160 g) brown rice flour

—————

YIELD: 8 BURGERS

In a skillet, heat the 1 tablespoon (15 ml) olive oil and sauté the mushrooms and onion over medium-high heat for 7 to 10 minutes, or until fragrant, translucent, and reduced by half. Add the sautéed onion and mushrooms, tomato pieces, rice, pesto, and salt and pepper to taste to a food processor and pulse until well combined but still a little chunky. Transfer to a mixing bowl.

Depending on the moisture content of your mixture, knead in the flour a little at a time until a good consistency for forming patties is reached. Refrigerate for at least 20 minutes, so the flour can absorb the flavors and moisture of the mixture. Form into 8 patties and cook as desired.

If baking, use a baking sheet lined with parchment or a silicone baking mat, and bake at 350°F (180°C, or gas mark 4) for 15 minutes, and then flip and bake for 15 minutes longer, until firm and just beginning to brown. If frying, make sure there is enough oil in the pan to prevent it from sticking and fry over medium-high heat for 4 to 5 minutes per side, or until a nice golden crust forms.

You Are SO Vegan!

Have you ever made your own sun-dried tomatoes? It's very simple, but it does take a long time . . . and doesn't require any sun! Simply wash and halve tomatoes and gently rinse out the seeds. Place on a cookie sheet lined with parchment or silicone mat, and bake at 200°F (95°C) until the desired consistency it reached. They should be dry to the touch, and leathery in texture, but still pliable. This could take 8 to 10 hours (or more). When ready, cool before storing in an airtight container in the refrigerator.

POTATO SAMOSA BURGER

Gluten-Free Soy-Free Nut Free No-Sugar Added

I could totally sit on the couch, cuddled up under a warm blanket in my fuzzy slippers, bingewatching reruns of Supernatural, while popping samosa after samosa in my mouth. This burger is just like the real thing . . . sans the crust! Enjoy as you would any samosa. I like to have mine with a side of traditional chana masala and saffron rice.

1½ pounds (682 g) russet potatoes, washed (peeled if desired)

1 cup (160 g) diced onion

1 teaspoon ground ginger

1 teaspoon ground coriander

1 teaspoon garam masala

1 teaspoon ground cumin

1 hot green chile pepper, such as a jalapeño, seeded and diced

3 tablespoons (45 ml) sesame oil

1½ cups (200 g) fresh or frozen green peas

Olive oil, for frying

YIELD: 6 TO 8 BURGERS

Bring a large pot of water to a boil. Cut the potatoes into chunks about 1 inch (2.5 cm). I like to leave the skins on, but that's your call. Boil the potatoes until fork-tender. Drain and return to the pot.

Add the onion, ginger, coriander, garam masala, cumin, chile pepper, and sesame oil and mash with a hand masher or your hands. Carefully mix in the peas, trying not to smash them too much.

Form into 6 to 8 patties.

Panfry in plenty of oil for 3 to 5 minutes per side, or until a nice golden crispy crust forms.

You Are SO Vegan!

Instead of forming these into patties, form them into log shapes around a skewer and fry as directed above. Serve in a pita with hummus and spinach, drizzled with Tangy Tahini Sauce (page 189).

ENCHILADA BURGER

No-Sugar Added *Gluten-Free*

Way lower in fat and way less work than traditional enchiladas! Serve topped with Nondairy Sour Cream (page 198) and green onions on a nice warm corn tortilla with some Cilantro Lime Rice (page 227).

---

2 cups (470 ml) enchilada sauce

1 cup (160 g) diced onion

1 cup (96 g) TVP granules

⅓ cup (46 g) chopped black olives

¼ cup (24 g) chopped green onions

1 cup (114 g) masa harina flour (I like Maseca brand)

½ cup (120 g) nondairy sour cream, store-bought or homemade (page 198)

5 slices jarred jalapeños, chopped

Oil, for frying (optional)

YIELD: 6 BURGERS

In a large stockpot, bring the enchilada sauce and diced onion to a boil.

Stir in the TVP granules. Remove from the heat, cover, and let sit for 10 minutes.

Add the olives, green onions, flour, sour cream, and jalapeños and knead until everything is well incorporated.

Form into 6 patties. Cook as desired. It's good both ways!

Panfry in oil for 3 to 5 minutes per side, or until golden brown and crispy. Or, bake in the oven at 350°F (180°C, or gas mark 4), on a baking sheet lined with parchment or a silicone baking mat, for about 15 minutes per side, until firm and just beginning to brown. Alternatively, Air-Fry for 16–18 minutes at 375°F (190°C).

You Are SO Vegan!

Go bananas and add in 6 ounces (120 g) soy-chorizo to the dough before making them into patties!

BLACK BEAN TAMALE BURGER WITH MOLE SAUCE

Gluten-Free

Nut Free

Soy-Free

This burger can be baked or fried with great results. The mole sauce is a simplified version of a Mexican classic that normally takes hours to make. You only need about 1 cup (240 g) for the actual burgers, so use the remainder to pour over them or mix in with rice. Serve the patty on its own or on a warm corn tortilla with Cilantro Lime Rice (page 227) and fajita-grilled vegetables.

FOR MOLE SAUCE:

1½ tablespoons (23 ml) vegetable oil

½ cup (80 g) finely diced white or yellow onion

1½ tablespoons (23 g) finely chopped garlic

½ teaspoon dried oregano

1 teaspoon cumin

¼ teaspoon cinnamon

2 tablespoons (16 g) chili powder, or to taste

2¼ cups (530 ml) vegetable broth

1 teaspoon (1 g) instant coffee crystals or 1 tablespoon (15 ml) brewed espresso

1 tablespoon (8 g) cornstarch dissolved in 2 tablespoons (30 ml) water to make a slurry

½ disc (¼ ounce [21 g]) Mexican or dark chocolate

To make the mole sauce: Heat the oil in a skillet, add the onion and garlic, and sauté over medium heat until translucent, 5 to 7 minutes. Add the oregano, cumin, and cinnamon and cook for about 5 minutes longer.

Mix in the chili powder to taste, then slowly stir in the broth. Bring to a boil. Reduce the heat to a simmer.

Add the coffee crystals, or espresso, and cornstarch slurry, stir well, and continue to simmer until reduced and thickened, about 20 minutes.

Remove from the heat and stir in the chocolate until melted.

FOR BURGERS:

3 cups (342 g) masa harina flour (I like Maseca brand)

1 cup (235 ml) oil

1 cup (235 ml) Mole Sauce

½ cup (120 ml) water

1 can [15 ounces (425 g)] black or pinto beans, drained and rinsed

1 teaspoon cumin

1 teaspoon oregano

½ teaspoon cayenne pepper

Salt and pepper

Oil, for frying (optional)

———————

YIELD: 8 BURGERS

To make the burgers: In a mixing bowl, combine all the ingredients and knead until well incorporated.

Form into 8 patties and cook as desired. Panfry in plenty of oil for 4 to 5 minutes per side, or until golden brown and crispy; Air-Fry at 375°F (190°C) for 16 to 18 minutes; or bake in the oven at 350°F (180°C, or gas mark 4), on a baking sheet lined with parchment or a silicone baking mat, covered in a foil tent, for about 10 minutes per side.

You Are SO Vegan!

For an even more tamale-like burger, steam bake in cornhusks! You will need 10 large cornhusks, soaked in warm water for at least 1 hour. Set aside 8 intact cornhusks and cut the remaining 2 cornhusks into strips. Take 1 intact cornhusk and place it on the counter with the pointy side facing away from you. Place the patty in the center of the husk. Fold the pointy end over the patty, toward you. Then fold each side of the remaining three sides of the husk over the patty and secure by tying with a strip of cornhusk. Repeat with the remaining 7 patties. Place seam side down on the baking sheet and bake in the oven at 350°F (180°C, or gas mark 4) for 20 minutes. No need to flip.

EDAMAME BURGER

Yep, green burgers. This recipe makes a lot, but they freeze well, so you can have green burgers all week long! Serve bunless with a side of Baked Sweet Potato Fries (page 216, and pictured here) and Chipotle Dipping Sauce (page 192); or, serve on a soft white roll with the traditional burger fixin's.

---

2 cups (340 g) shelled and frozen edamame

1 can (15 ounces [425 g]) chickpeas, with liquid

8 ounces (227 g) sliced mushrooms

½ cup (65 g) finely ground raw cashews

½ cup (60 g) nutritional yeast

4 cloves garlic

½ teaspoon ground cumin

¼ teaspoon liquid smoke (optional)

1 teaspoon gluten-free tamari

Salt and pepper, to taste

3½ cups (420 g) chickpea flour

Oil, for frying (optional)

YIELD: 16 BURGERS

Place the frozen edamame and the entire can of chickpeas, including the liquid, in a saucepot and warm through. This step is to defrost the edamame; if you use fresh or precooked edamame, you can skip this step.

Combine the edamame, chickpeas and liquid, mushrooms, cashews, yeast, garlic, cumin, liquid smoke, tamari, and salt and pepper in a food processor and process until smooth. Pour into a large bowl.

Slowly add the flour until a thicker consistency is formed. Depending on the moisture content of your mixture, you may need just a little flour or a whole lot.

Place the entire bowl in the refrigerator for 20 to 30 minutes to stiffen up and make it easier to handle when forming the patties. Form into 16 patties.

Heat the oil in a sauté pan and fry the patties for 4 to 5 minutes, or until golden brown on both sides. Alternatively, use your Air-Fryer at 375°F (190°C) for 16 to 18 minutes.

You Are SO Vegan!

Don't dare throw that bean water down the drain! Aquafaba (a.k.a. the liquid from a can of beans, most commonly chickpeas) is liquid gold! It can be whipped up like egg whites and used in all sorts of amazing recipes from French macarons, to the Vegan Mayo on page 197! Store it by pouring it into ice-cube trays and then transferring to a resealable freezer bag.

MOO GOO GAI PAN BURGER

This burger is full of exotic flavor and ingredients. It creates quite a delightful aroma when you make it, so don't be surprised when everyone in the house wanders into the kitchen while you're cooking! I like these served solo on a bed of cabbage (steamed or raw) topped with a dollop of spicy Chinese mustard and hot ketchup. On the side? Sticky or fried rice.

2 tablespoons (30 ml) sesame oil

8 ounces (227 g) sliced mushrooms

5 ounces (140 g) sliced bamboo shoots

5 ounces (140 g) sliced water chestnuts

3½ tablespoons (28 g) chopped or grated fresh ginger

2 tablespoons (30 g) minced garlic

Salt and pepper

⅔ cup (160 ml) gluten-free tamari

⅓ cup (80 ml) rice wine vinegar

2 tablespoons (16 g) cornstarch dissolved in ¼ cup (60 ml) water to make a slurry

4 cups (700 g) cooked sushi rice

1 cup (160 g) white rice flour

¼ cup (64 g) tahini paste

Oil, for frying (optional)

———

YIELD: 8 BURGERS

Preheat a wok or large frying pan, then add the sesame oil and heat. Add the mushrooms, bamboo shoots, water chestnuts, ginger, and garlic. Add a pinch of salt. Sauté until the mushrooms have reduced in size by about half, 7 to 10 minutes. Add the tamari and vinegar, bring to a boil, slowly add the cornstarch slurry, and remove from the heat.

Add the rice, rice flour, tahini, and salt and pepper to taste and mix well. Let rest for about 20 minutes. The mixture will be sticky.

Meanwhile, preheat the oven to 350°F (180°C, or gas mark 4). Line a baking sheet with parchment or a silicone baking mat.

Form the mixture into 8 patties and place on the prepared baking sheet.

Bake, covered in foil, for 30 minutes, flipping halfway through. For an extra-crispy crust, panfry in a bit of oil for 2 to 3 minutes per side, after baking.

You Are SO Vegan!

Scramble up some crumbled tofu by panfrying in a bit of oil with a sprinkle of garlic powder, onion powder, and turmeric for color. Cook until warmed all the way through. Stir in a squirt of Dijon mustard and a pinch of Kala Namak (black salt) for an eggy flavor. Use this quick scramble to add to fried rice!

THAI-INSPIRED BLACK BEAN TOFU AND POTATO PATTIES

These are really spicy, but you can cool them down a bit by reducing the red pepper flakes by half without changing the intended flavor. Me? I like 'em spicy.

4 red potatoes (about 1¼ pounds [193 g])

12 ounces (340 g) extra-firm tofu, drained and pressed

1 can (15 ounces [425 g]) black beans, drained and rinsed

¼ cup (64 g) peanut butter

½ cup (48 g) finely chopped scallions

1 to 2 tablespoons (15 to 30 g) dried red pepper flakes

2 tablespoons (30 g) minced garlic

1 teaspoon green curry paste

1 teaspoon Sriracha sauce

¼ teaspoon dried ground coriander

Salt and pepper

¼ cup (40 g) rice flour

YIELD: 10 BURGERS

Preheat the oven to 350°F (180°C, or gas mark 4). Have ready a nonstick baking sheet.

Bring a pot of salted water to a boil.

Cut the potatoes into approximately 1-inch (2.5 cm) chunks, leaving the skin on.

Place the potatoes in the boiling water and let boil for 10 to 12 minutes, or until fork-tender. Drain and set aside to cool.

Meanwhile, crumble the tofu into a mixing bowl, and add the beans, peanut butter, scallions, red pepper flakes, garlic, curry paste, Sriracha sauce, coriander, and salt and pepper to taste.

When the potatoes are cool enough to handle, add them to the tofu mixture, and knead together with your hands until everything is well combined. Depending on the moistness of your mix, add more or less of the ¼ cup (40 g) flour.

Form into 10 patties, place on the baking sheet, and cover with foil. Bake for 15 minutes per side, or until crispy.

You Are SO Vegan!

Tuck it into a gluten-free bun on a bed of shredded cabbage and slather with Thai Peanut Sauce (page 199). Serve with a side of Thai-style peanut coleslaw.

COCONUT RUM RICE BURGER

Inspired by the folks that enjoy a "seriously easygoing" lifestyle in Barbados. But don't let the innocent name fool you! This burger packs a spicy punch, so feel free to cut down the amount of Sriracha if you want the sweet flavors to poke through a bit more.

FOR RICE:

4 cups (940 ml) water

2 cups (360 g) uncooked jasmine rice

1 tablespoon (15 ml) white rice vinegar

1 tablespoon (21 g) agave nectar

¼ teaspoon salt

FOR BURGERS:

1 recipe rice (above)

½ cup (120 ml) orange juice

1 cup (235 ml) coconut-flavored rum

½ cup (65 g) crushed macadamia nuts

1 tablespoon (15 g) minced garlic

1 cup (160 g) diced white onion

2 tablespoons (34 g) Sriracha sauce

1 cup (112 g) coconut flour

½ cup (120 ml) coconut oil, for frying

YIELD: 8 TO 10 BURGERS

To make the rice: The easiest way is to throw all of those ingredients into a rice cooker and let it do the work. If you don't have a rice cooker, in a pot with a tight-fitting lid, bring the water to a boil. Add the rice, vinegar, agave, and salt. Stir, lower the heat to a simmer, cover, and cook for 20 to 25 minutes, or until the rice is tender and the liquid is absorbed. Stir occasionally to prevent scorching and sticking to the bottom of the pot.

Transfer the rice to a large mixing bowl and let cool.

To make the burgers: Combine the rice and remaining burger ingredients and mix well. Knead together until a patty-able consistency is reached. If necessary, add a little more flour.

Form into 8 to 10 patties.

Preheat a frying pan with the coconut oil over medium-high heat.

Panfry each burger for 3 to 5 minutes per side, or until a nice golden crispy crust forms.

You Are SO Vegan!

Grill up some pineapple rings and bell peppers and serve with these burgers, bunless, over a bed of crisp raw cabbage.

MASA MASALA BURGER

Gluten-Free *Nut Free* *No-Sugar Added* *Soy-Free*

Two of my favorite cuisines are Mexican and Indian, so why not join the two in a burger? Genius, I say! Serve on a Sweet Potato Bun (page 211, pictured here) alongside a nice big pile of brown rice, lentils, and peas mixed with some Tangy Tahini Sauce (page 198), as shown here.

---

1 cup (114 g) masa harina flour (I like Maseca brand)

1 cup (198 g) fully cooked lentils

⅔ cup (160 ml) water

2 tablespoons (30 ml) olive oil, plus more for frying (optional)

1 teaspoon garam masala

½ teaspoon cumin

⅛ teaspoon sea salt

Freshly cracked black pepper

YIELD: 4 BURGERS

This couldn't be easier. Mix all the ingredients together and form into 4 patties.

Panfry in oil (or you can use a little nonstick spray on a hot skillet) and fry for 3 to 5 minutes per side. Alternatively, use your Air-Fryer at 365°F (185°C) for 16 to 18 minutes. You can also bake these, but they tend to dry out a bit, so be sure to use a foil tent and maybe even brush a little extra olive oil on them before baking. Bake at 350°F (180°C, or gas mark 4) for about 10 minutes per side.

You Are SO Vegan!

Bring it back down south of the border by serving topped with a pile of pinto or black beans, and a big dollop of Mom's Mango Salsa (page 200).

THREE PEPPER STIR-FRY BURGER

Gluten-Free

Soy-Free

If you have a wok, this is a good time to use it. If not, use your largest frying pan or even a stockpot.

---

2 tablespoons (30 ml) mild-flavored vegetable oil

2 cups (320 g) diced red onion

8 ounces (227 g) mushrooms, chopped

1 red bell pepper, cored, seeded, and diced

1 yellow bell pepper, cored, seeded, and diced

1 green bell pepper, cored, seeded, and diced

3 cups (522 g) cooked brown rice

2 tablespoons (32 g) peanut butter

3 tablespoons (45 ml) sesame oil

1 teaspoon cumin

1 tablespoon (17 g) Sriracha sauce

3 tablespoons (24 g) arrowroot powder

YIELD: 8 BURGERS

Preheat a wok, add the oil to heat, then add the onion, mushrooms, and bell peppers. Stir-fry over high heat for about 10 minutes, stirring often, until the vegetables have reduced in volume by about half. Remove from the heat.

Stir in the rice, peanut butter, sesame oil, cumin, Sriracha, and arrowroot powder. Mix well.

Refrigerate for at least 20 minutes to thicken up a bit. You can refrigerate overnight, if desired.

Preheat the oven to 350°F (180°C, or gas mark 4). Line a baking sheet with parchment or a silicone baking mat, or spray with nonstick spray.

Form the mixture into 8 patties and place on the prepared baking sheet.

Bake, uncovered, for 15 to 20 minutes, then gently flip and bake 15 to 20 minutes longer, until firm and just beginning to brown. Remove from the oven and let sit for about 10 minutes before serving.

You Are SO Vegan!

Serve these up bunless on a nice big leaf of purple cabbage with some Thai Peanut Sauce (page 199).

FIRE-ROASTED RED PEPPER BURGER

Gluten-Free   Nut Free   Soy-Free   No-Sugar Added

Über-Super-Mega-Awesome Tester Liz Wyman had a burger at a restaurant that she loved and asked me to try and recreate it. This one's for Liz. Serve on a crusty whole wheat bun or tucked inside pita, garnished with fresh greens and a goddess-type dressing.

1 can (15 ounces [425 g]) chickpeas, with liquid

3 or 4 cloves garlic

1 red bell pepper

2 tablespoons (32 g) tahini paste

2 tablespoons (30 ml) sesame oil

2 tablespoons (30 ml) lemon juice

Salt and pepper

2 cups (240 g) chickpea flour

Oil, for frying (optional)

YIELD: 4 BURGERS

Empty the can of chickpeas, along with the liquid, into a saucepan, add the garlic, bring to a boil, lower the heat to a simmer, and simmer for 15 to 20 minutes.

While the beans are simmering, roast the bell pepper. Using tongs, place the entire pepper on an open flame. Your gas stove burner works perfect for this. Roast it until it is blackened and soft. Let cool and remove the seeds and stem. Peel off the skins, if desired. I like to leave them on, because the nice charred bits add a lovely smokiness to the burger.

After the beans are done simmering, strain out the liquid, reserving the garlic. To a food processor or blender, add the beans, garlic, seeded fire-roasted pepper, tahini, sesame oil, lemon juice, and salt and pepper to taste. Blend until smooth. Transfer to a bowl and add the flour, ½ cup (60 g) at a time, until a patty-able consistency is reached. Depending on the moisture content of your beans and pepper, more or less flour may be needed.

Form into 4 patties and cook as desired. Fry in oil for 3 to 5 minutes per side, or until golden brown and crispy; Air-Fry at 375°F (190°C) for 16 to 18 minutes; or bake on a baking sheet lined with parchment or a silicone baking mat at 350°F (180°C, or gas mark 4) for 15 to 20 minutes per side, covered in a foil tent to retain moisture, until firm and warmed all the way through.

You Are SO Vegan!

Make a quick Goddess Dressing by blending Aquafaba Mayo (page 197) with fresh cilantro, parsley, tarragon, green onions, dill, and garlic.

BABA GHANOUSH BURGER

Nut Free Gluten-Free No-Sugar Added

Baba ghanoush is traditionally a paste made from eggplant, garlic, cumin, and spices. It is traditionally used as a spread or dip with flatbreads or crackers. In some countries, cooks add onions and tahini to the mix. For this recipe, I incorporated them right into the burger. This burger would be perfect on flatbread or in a pita. Hummus makes a nice spread, as does the Garlic Artichoke Spread (page 194).

---

2 tablespoons (30 ml) sesame oil

12 ounces (340 g) peeled and cubed eggplant

2 tablespoons (30 g) minced garlic

8 ounces (227 g) diced onion

1 teaspoon cumin

Salt and pepper

1 cup (198 g) cooked green or black lentils

1 cup (120 g) chickpea flour

Oil, for frying (optional)

YIELD: 4 TO 6 BURGERS

Preheat the sesame oil in a skillet over medium-high heat. Add the eggplant, cook for about 5 minutes.

Add the garlic, diced onion, cumin, and salt and pepper to taste. Cook for 15 minutes, uncovered, turning occasionally. Remove from heat.

Stir in the lentils and sprinkle in the flour. Mix very well.

Cover and refrigerate for at least 30 minutes, or even until the next day. The longer you leave it in the fridge, the more the flour will absorb the flavors of the mixture. In addition, refrigeration helps make the patties easier to form.

Preheat the oven to 350°F (180°C, or gas mark 4).

Form into 4 to 6 patties. Bake, uncovered, for 20 minutes, or until firm and just beginning to brown. Then, if desired, fry in oil for 2 to 3 minutes per side, until a nice golden crust forms. Alternatively, use your Air-Fryer at 375°F (190°C) for 16 to 18 minutes.

You Are SO Vegan!

Skip the bun and serve on top of a nice big pile of Taboulleh Salad (page 109) as shown here, and add a big dollop of Tzatziki Sauce (page 199) up on top.

CHORIZO AND EGG BURGER

Gluten-Free

Nut Free

The first time I had a traditional Mexican breakfast was when I was about thirteen years old. I spent the night at my girlfriend Yvette's house and was served up beans and rice with tortillas. No forks. I was totally intrigued and obviously uneducated in the ways of Mexican culture. I've come a long way since then!

FOR MEXIMEET:

1 cup (96 g) TVP granules

2 tablespoons (14 g) paprika

1 teaspoon ground cumin

1 teaspoon sugar

1 teaspoon garlic powder

1 teaspoon onion powder

½ teaspoon cayenne pepper

½ teaspoon chili powder

½ teaspoon chipotle powder

½ teaspoon salt

1 cup (235 ml) water or vegetable broth

½ cup (120 ml) mild-flavored vegetable oil

To make the MexiMeet: In a microwave-safe bowl, mix together the TVP granules and the spices. Add the water, cover tightly with plastic wrap, and microwave for 5 to 6 minutes. Alternatively, bring the water to a boil, pour over the TVP granules and spices, cover, and let stand for 10 minutes. While still hot, carefully mix in the oil.

To make the burgers: In a large, flat skillet, heat the 2 tablespoons (30 ml) oil over medium-high heat. Add the onion and sauté until just beginning to brown. Add the mustard powder, turmeric, garlic powder, onion powder, and salt and pepper to taste. Stir to combine.

Crumble in the tofu and continue to cook for about 5 more minutes. Remove from the heat. Stir in the MexiMeet and then the masa. Mix until crumbly and well incorporated. Let sit for about 20 minutes.

Form the mixture into 6 to 8 patties and panfry in additional oil for 3 to 5 minutes per side, or until a nice crispy crust forms. Alternatively, brush both sides of the patty with oil and use your Air-Fryer at 375°F (190°C) for 14 to 16 minutes.

You Are SO Vegan!

Serve with a side of frijoles and tortillas for an authentic Mexican breakfast. I like mine with some sour cream and a few slices of avocado (or guacamole). Use the MexiMeet as a taco or burrito filling, too!

FOR BURGERS:

2 tablespoons (30 ml) mild-flavored vegetable oil, plus extra for frying

1 cup (160 g) diced onion

1 tablespoon (8 g) mustard powder

½ teaspoon turmeric

1 teaspoon garlic powder

1 teaspoon onion powder

Salt and pepper

12 ounces (340 g) extra-firm tofu, drained and pressed

1 recipe MexiMeet (above)

½ cup (62 g) masa flour (I like Maseca brand)

———

YIELD: 6 TO 8 BURGERS

Chapter 10

FAST FOOD FAVORITES

Craving a Baconator or a Big Mac?
I've got you covered.

THE BETTER MAC

Here you go, Micky Dees, I fixed the song for you! "Two all vegan patties, Better Sauce, lettuce, cheeze, pickles, onions, on a sesame seed bun!" Ahh, the Big Mac. A shimmering icon of the good ol' US of A. Excess at its finest. (I'm talking to you, extra bun in the middle.)

---

4 sesame seed buns

Vegan butter, optional

½ cup Better Sauce (opposite page) prepared

1 cup (72 g) shredded iceberg lettuce

½ cup (80 g) finely diced white onion

4 beef-y type burger patties, such as the All-American Burger (page 38) or the Really Meaty Burger (page 39), prepared

2 slices of your favorite American-style vegan cheese

10 slices of dill pickle

———

YIELD: 2 BURGERS

Separate the buns, set aside or discard two top buns, leaving you with two tops and four bottoms. Lightly butter each bun, if desired, and toast in a dry skillet until lightly browned.

Spread all buns with a thick layer of Better Sauce.

Pile shredded lettuce evenly on all four bun bottoms.

Sprinkle diced onion evenly on top of all of the lettuce shreds.

Place a burger patty on two of the burger bottoms.

Place a slice of cheese on each of the two burgers.

Place the remaining two bun bottoms on top of the cheese, lettuce side up.

Place remaining burger patties on top.

Top burger patties with five slices of pickle each.

Complete the burger with the two remaining top buns and serve.

You Are SO Vegan!

Replace the shredded iceberg lettuce with shredded dino lacinato (dinosaur) kale and replace the Better Sauce with Creamy Sesame Sriracha Sauce (page 200).

BETTER SAUCE

What's so special about mixing together ketchup, mayo, and pickle relish anyway? This version of "special sauce" has a few added ingredients to this classic burger staple that make it just a little bit, well, better.!

½ cup (112 g) vegan mayo, store-bought or homemade (page 197)

2 tablespoons (34 g) ketchup

2 tablespoons (30 g) dill or sweet pickle relish

1 teaspoon stone ground or whole grain mustard

1 teaspoon minced garlic

½ teaspoon onion powder

½ teaspoon dried dill (or 1½ teaspoons fresh)

Salt and pepper, to taste

—————

YIELD: JUST OVER ½ CUP (135 ML)

Whisk all ingredients together until well combined. Store in the refrigerator in an airtight container for up to a week, until ready to use.

You Are SO Vegan!

Looking for an oil- free version of this sauce? Replace the vegan mayo with silken tofu.

COWGIRL BACON CHEESEBURGER

Carl's Jr. (Hardee's in other parts of the country) once had an ad campaign, "If it doesn't get all over the place, it doesn't belong in your face!" This was usually accompanied by a scantily clad woman, devouring a big messy burger, sometimes while lying on the hood of a car, or in a laundromat, or just sitting there in front of the camera in a studio. The BBQ sauce would almost always drip onto her shirt in a suggestive manner. The commercials were just bizarre. But, whatevs. I'm taking back their signature Western Bacon Cheeseburger and giving it a (vegan) cowgirl's attitude. It's big. It's messy. And you don't even have to strip naked to eat it! Flash forward to 2019 . . . Carl's Jr. offers the Beyond Meaty Patty, and you can substitute it on ANY of their burgers for an upcharge. Vegan burgers at a drive-thru? Yes please!

---

4 sesame seed buns

1 cup (235 ml) Strawberry BBQ Sauce
(page 191)

1 recipe Baked Onion Rings
(page 223), divided

4 Sunday Afternoon Grillers
(page 35), prepared

1 cup (235 ml) Noochy Cheesy Sauce
page 110)

8 slices Bacon Strips (page 202)

YIELD: 4 BURGERS

To assemble each burger, start by lightly toasting the buns. On the bottom bun, add 2 tablespoons (30 ml) Strawberry BBQ Sauce, then add 2 to 3 onion rings right on top of the sauce. Next, add the patty, then add ¼ cup (60 ml) cheesy sauce. (I told you it was going to be messy!) Then add 2 slices of Bacon Strips. Top with another 2 tablespoons (30 ml) BBQ sauce and finish it with the top half of the bun.

Serve with remaining onion rings on the side.

You Are SO Vegan!

Double up on the western bacon-y goodness by subbing the Western Bacon Cheeseburgers (page 36) for the patties.

DOUBLE UP

Out here in California we have In-N-Out Burger with its iconic crisscrossed palm trees in front of every restaurant, and bible verses on the bottom of every cup. (It's true!) They have an almost cult-like following with secret menu items (including a vegan option!) and die-hard fans, who, once they move out of Cali, complain of In-N-Out withdrawal. Their signature sandwich is a Double-Double. But we aren't stopping there. We are going full animal-style on this one.

FOR THE MUSTARD GRILLED PATTIES:

1 recipe All-American Burgers (page 38), prepared as directed below

¼ cup (60 ml) yellow mustard

Oil, for frying

FOR THE GRILLED ONIONS:

1 tablespoon (15 ml) mild- flavored vegetable oil

1 large white or yellow onion, diced

½ teaspoon salt

Water, as needed

FOR EACH BURGER:

1 soft white bun, store-bought or homemade (page 206), toasted

2 tablespoons (30 ml) Better Sauce (page 159)

4 slices of dill pickle

1 slice tomato

¼ cup (60 ml) Cheezy Sauce (page 183)

Grilled Onions (above)

2 Mustard Grilled Patties

1 leaf romaine or green leaf lettuce

YIELD: 2 BURGERS

To make the mustard grilled patties: Follow the burger recipe as directed up until the cooking instructions. To cook, heat oil in a frying pan or skillet over medium-high heat. Prior to adding the patties to the pan, coat each patty with 1 tablespoon (15 ml) of yellow mustard using your hands. Add to the pan and fry for 4 to 5 minutes per side.

To make the grilled onions: Reduce heat to medium-low. Add oil to the pan to preheat. Add onions, and salt, toss to coat. Cook, tossing and stirring every so often until the onions are translucent and browned, about 15 minutes. Once onions begin to look dry, add 1 tablespoon (15 ml) water to the pan and stir. Continue cooking until the water evaporates and onions start sizzling again. Repeat, adding 1 tablespoon (15 ml) of water each time until onions are dark brown and super soft, about three times total.

To assemble the burgers: Slather Better Sauce onto the bottom bun and layer on the pickles, tomato, and lettuce, and 1 Mustard Grilled Patty.

In a small bowl, mix together cheezy sauce and grilled onions. Place half of the cheezy onion mixture on top of the patty, then add the second patty and pour the remaining cheezy onion mixture on top. Finish with the top bun and serve immediately.

You Are SO Vegan!

Serve this burger up with a side of animal-style Fries. Top your fries with cheezy sauce, chopped grilled onions, and a generous pour-over of Better Sauce.

DOUBLE DOWN

KFC (formerly known as Kentucky Fried Chicken) released the Double-Down in 2010. It was an instant hit, both as a failure and as a success! This gluttonous, yet somehow intriguing, sandwich has no bun. Instead of a bun, two fried chicken breasts sandwich two slices of bacon, pepper jack cheese, and the Colonel's Special Sauce. It was just screaming to be veganized.

FOR THE CLUCK'N PECKS:

1 ½ cups (216 g) vital wheat gluten flour

½ cup (60 g) chickpea flour

¼ cup (30 g) nutritional yeast

1 tablespoon (1 g) dried parsley

2 teaspoons (6 g) onion powder

1 teaspoon garlic powder

1 teaspoon dried oregano

½ teaspoon salt

½ teaspoon ground celery seed

11 ½ cups (2.7 L) vegan chicken-flavored broth, store-bought or homemade (page 104), divided

FOR THE CRISPY COATING:

1 cup (125 g) all-purpose flour

1 teaspoon dried parsley

½ teaspoon garlic powder

½ teaspoon onion powder

½ teaspoon dried mustard

¼ teaspoon smoked paprika

¼ teaspoon salt

¼ teaspoon black pepper

1 cup (235 ml) soymilk

2 tablespoons (30 ml) lemon juice

Oil, for frying

To make the pecks: In a medium-size mixing bowl, mix together all ingredients except broth. Add in 1½ cups of the broth and knead until a wet and elastic dough is formed. Allow to sit for 15 minutes to allow gluten to develop.

Divide into 8 equal portions and flatten each portion into a cutlet shape. Allow to rest an additional 10 minutes.

While resting, place remaining 10 cups (2.35 L) of broth in a pot.

Carefully add each cutlet into the pot, and bring to a boil, reduce to a gentle simmer, and simmer for 1 hour, returning. Returning occasionally to give a stir.

Remove from heat. To keep moist, store in an airtight container, covered in broth, in the refrigerator, until ready to use.

To make the crispy coating: Mix together flour and spices mixture in a shallow dish. Mix together soymilk and lemon juice in a separate small bowl. It will curdle and become like buttermilk.

Dip one peck cutlet in the flour mixture to lightly coat, then dip in buttermilk mixture then back into the flour mixture, and for a thicker coat.

To fry the pecks, preheat the oil in your deep fryer, or fill a frying pan with about an inch of oil, and heat it on high heat.

Place in oil and fry for about 2 to 3 minutes or until golden and crispy. (If you are using the frying pan method, you will need to flip after about 2 minutes and repeat on the other side.) Transfer to a plate lined with paper towels to absorb excess oil. Repeat with remaining 7 pieces.

FOR THE SASSY SAUCE:

½ cup (112 g) vegan mayonnaise, store-bought or homemade (page 197)

2 tablespoons (35 g) ketchup

2 tablespoon (35 g) Sriracha sauce

1 teaspoon dried chives or parsley

FOR EACH SANDWICH:

2 Fried Cluck'n Pecks, prepared

2 slices Bacon Strips (page 202), prepared

2 slices Nutty-Pepper Jack (page 115), prepared

2½ tablespoons (23 g) Sassy Sauce, prepared

YIELD: 4 BURGERS

To make the sassy sauce: Whisk together sauce ingredients in a small bowl.

To assemble the sandwiches: Spread a thick layer of sauce on 1 piece of fried peck, then place 2 pieces of bacon, then 1 slice Pepper Jack, and then top with another piece of peck spread with sauce.

You Are SO Vegan!

No doubt, there is a whole lot of labor involved in making this recipe from scratch. Here's a timesaving tip: Use store-bought ingredients! Gardein makes a great vegan chicken breast (find it in the frozen section of most supermarkets), Follow Your Heart makes a near-perfect vegan Pepper Jack cheese and Vegenaise. Now all you have to do is fry up the chicken and whisk together the sauce. Easy-peasy!

FILET WITHOUT FISH

This particular "burger" is such a weird, yet iconic, fast food favorite, that I just had to include a second entry from McDonalds in this chapter. The Filet-O-Fish is a fried fish filet patty on a soft white bun toped with HALF of a slice of American cheese and a dollop of tartar sauce. I've always wondered how this quirky menu item has survived the test of time, but, then again, I should know better than to be surprised by humans. My spin on this classic is far from true to the original. The patty is a rice-and-seaweed concoction that is not deep fried, but rather formed into a cake right on the griddle. Serve with tartar sauce, but definitely skip the cheese on this one. Top this with pickled veggies (page 54).

FOR THE FISH:

1 cup (180 g) uncooked long grain rice, such as basmati or jasmine

2 cups (470 ml) water

1 tablespoon (3 g) hijiki seaweed

½ teaspoon salt, or to taste

¼ teaspoon cumin

⅛ teaspoon red chili flakes, or to taste

Oil, for frying (optional)

FOR THE TARTAR SAUCE:

¾ cup (168 g) Aquafaba Mayo (page 197)

1 tablespoon (15 g) sweet pickle relish

1 teaspoon lemon juice

½ teaspoon minced garlic

½ teaspoon onion powder

¼ teaspoon dried dill, or ¾ teaspoon fresh

YIELD: 6 BURGERS AND 1 CUP (235 ML) TARTAR SAUCE

To make the fish: Stir together all ingredients in the bowl of your rice cooker and cook according to machine instructions. If you do not have a rice cooker, add water and seaweed to a pot with a tight-fitting lid. Bring to a boil, stir in rice and spices to the boiling water, reduce to a simmer, cover, and simmer for 15 to 20 minutes, until fluffy and tender. Make tartar sauce while rice is cooking.

To make the tartar sauce: Mix together all ingredients and keep refrigerated until ready to use.

Once rice is cooked, heat a small amount of oil, if using, in a frying pan or skillet over medium-high heat. Using a large ice-cream scoop, drop about ¾ cup (146 g) of the rice mixture onto the pan and press flat with a spatula. Fry until browned, flip, and repeat on other side.

Serve on a soft bun with tartar sauce.

You Are SO Vegan!

If you really want to imitate the original, Gardein makes a frozen fishless filet that will make this task quite an easy one. Follow Your Heart brand makes a pretty incredible American-style cheese slice that will melt perfectly over the filets. Simply pop 'em in the oven according to package instructions and you'll have your own weird little fish-and-cheese sandwich in no time.

THE FAKE-O-NATOR!

Wendy's has this burger called the Baconator. It's got two square patties, SIX slices of bacon, two slices of American cheese, ketchup, and mayo. Want a vegan version? No problem!

1 recipe **All-American Burgers** (page 38), prepared dough

Oil, for frying

4 **Soft White Buns**, store-bought or homemade (page 206), toasted

½ cup (60 ml) **Cheezy Sauce** (page 183)

12 slices **Bacon Strips** (page 202)

2 tablespoons (34 g) ketchup

¼ cup (56 g) **vegan mayo**, store-bought or homemade (page 197)

YIELD: 2 BURGERS

Line a baking sheet with parchment.

To make the burgers, prepare the All-American Burger recipe as directed up until it says to form into patties.

Instead of forming into patties, press dough onto the baking sheet forming a square. Top with another sheet of parchment, and, using a rolling pin, roll smooth to achieve an 8x8-inch (20x20 cm) square. Remove top layer of parchment and cut the square into four equal 4x4-inch (10x10 cm) patties.

Preheat a small amount of oil in a pan or skillet over medium-high heat. Fry for 4 to 5 minutes per side, or Air-Fry at 375°F (190°C) for 13 to 15 minutes.

To assemble the burgers, add one patty directly onto the bottom half of one bun. Top with 2 tablespoons (30 ml) cheezy sauce and 3 slices of bacon. Repeat with a second patty. Add 1 tablespoon (17 g) of ketchup on top of the second patty. Spread a thick layer, about 2 tablespoons (28 g), vegan mayo on the top half of the bun and place on top.

Serve immediately.

You Are SO Vegan!

Make rice paper bacon! Use the marinade in the Bacon Strips recipe (page 202) and place in a dish. You will also need: a few pieces of rice paper, cut into bacon-size strips, a dish of hot (not boiling) water, a frying pan, and a plate lined with paper towels. Preheat the pan over medium-high heat. Carefully layer two strips of rice paper together and dip them in the hot water briefly. Smooth off excess liquid with your fingers. Dip softened strips into the marinade. Smooth off excess liquid with your fingers and transfer to the frying pan. Fry until browned and wrinkled, but still a tad flexible (overcooking will make it bitter). Transfer to towel-lined plate to crisp up.

THIS BACON CHEESEBURGER IS THE ULTIMATE

Not gonna lie, the Jack In the Box Bacon Ultimate Cheeseburger was my go-to fast food burger in my pregan days. Two juicy, fatty patties, American AND Swiss cheese, three slices of bacon, mayo, mustard, and ketchup on a soft buttery white bun. When this burger was first introduced, it was served on a sesame seed bun with an Onion Mayo Sauce, not plain old mayo. So, that's how we're gonna make it here. From what I can still remember, it was that onion mayo that really made it stand out.

FOR THE ONION MAYO SAUCE:

12 ounces (340 g) soft silken tofu

¾ cup (180 ml) mild-flavored vegetable oil

¼ cup (53 g) caramelized white onion

2 tablespoons (30 ml) apple cider vinegar

1 tablespoon (10 g) minced garlic

1 teaspoon Dijon mustard

½ teaspoon salt

FOR THE BURGERS:

1 recipe Really Meaty Burger (page 39) made into 8 patties

4 Sesame Seed Buns

8 slices vegan American-style cheese (I love the Follow Your Heart brand!)

4 slices vegan Swiss-style cheese

12 slices Bacon Strips (page 202)

4 tablespoons (68 g) ketchup

1 tablespoon plus 1 teaspoon (20 g) yellow mustard

½ cup (120 ml) Onion Mayo Sauce

To make the sauce: Add all ingredients to a blender and blend until silky smooth. Keep stored in an airtight container in the refrigerator; it will keep for at least two weeks.

To assemble the burgers: Start by adding one Really Meaty Burger patty directly on the bottom half of the bun. Do not toast the bun, just leave it in all of its soft white bread glory. Then add 1 slice of American-style Cheese and 1 slice of Swiss-style cheese. (Better layer those at an angle on top of each other for ultimate cheese coverage.) Then add another burger patty. Top that patty with another slice of American-style cheese, then layer on 3 slices of bacon strips. Add 1 tablespoon (17 g) ketchup and 1 teaspoon yellow mustard right on top of the bacon. Spread a generous 2 tablespoons (30 ml) Onion Mayo Sauce on the top half of the bun and place it on top.

Serve immediately.

YIELD: 4 BURGERS AND 1½ CUPS (355 ML) SAUCE

You Are SO Vegan!

Wanna make the Ultimate Bacon Ultimate Cheeseburger? Instead of using the Really Meaty Burger as the base for this one, use the BLT and Avocado Burger (page 41) with or without the avocado. (But, I mean, seriously, are you really gonna leave out the avocado?)

NOW THAT'S A WHOPPER!

Every fast food chain has its signature burger. During the first height of the burger wars in the 1980s it was always the Big Mac versus the Whopper. While they had similar ingredients (minus the gratuitous bun) the Whopper's claim to fame was that it was "flame-grilled" instead of fried. Notably, the Whopper doesn't come with cheese unless you ask for it, as in, a Whopper with Cheese. The Whopper is a pretty standard classic with the standard fixin's: lettuce, tomato, pickles, onions, ketchup, and mayo, on a sesame seed bun.

1 recipe Sunday Afternoon Grillers (page 35), prepared

6 sesame seed buns, toasted

24 slices of dill pickle

3 tablespoons (51 g) ketchup

1 white onion, sliced to ⅛-inch (3 mm) thick rounds

12 slices tomato

6 leaves green leaf lettuce

6 tablespoons (74 g) vegan mayo, store-bought or homemade (page 197)

———

YIELD: 6 BURGERS

This one is pretty self-explanatory. Assemble the sandwich by placing the cooked burger patty directly onto the bottom half of the bun. Add 4 slices of pickles to the top of the patty, taking care that they do not overlap. Using a squirt bottle (for maximum copycat effect) swirl 3 rings of ketchup on top of the pickles. Add 2 to 3 slices of onion, then 2 slices of tomato, then a leaf of lettuce. Finish it off by slathering 1 tablespoon (14 g) vegan mayo on the top half of the bun and placing it on top of the lettuce.

You Are SO Vegan!

Burger King actually has a veggie burger on its regular menu. Unfortunately, it is not vegan, as it contains egg. However, if you still want to pay homage to the King, you can order the French Toast Sticks that are accidentally vegan! And, unlike McDonalds, the French Fries at BK are also vegan. Yum!

WE'VE GOT NO MEAT!

I admit it. I used to love Arby's. The Roast Beef and Cheddar was a favorite of mine. Salty, gooey, fatty, and tasty. But then I learned about the horrors of factory farms. The lies. The greed. The torture. The abuse. I gave it up. Not just Arby's, but all animal products. For the animals. And for the planet.

FOR SPICED KETCHUP: (MY VERSION OF ARBY'S RED RANCH SAUCE)

1 cup (235 ml) ketchup

2 teaspoons water

1 tablespoon (14 g) dark brown sugar

1 tablespoon (15 ml) Sriracha sauce

1 teaspoon vegan Worcestershire sauce

¼ teaspoon garlic powder

¼ teaspoon onion powder

¼ teaspoon pepper

¼ teaspoon salt

FOR THE SANDWICHES:

2 cups (470 ml) water

½ cup (120 ml) soy sauce

¼ cup (60 ml) steak sauce

2 tablespoons (16 g) garlic powder

2 tablespoons (16 g) onion powder

½ teaspoon pepper

2 pounds (908 g) seitan, store-bought or homemade (page 203), sliced as thinly as possible

4 soft onion hamburger buns

2 tablespoons (28 g) nondairy butter

Spiced Ketchup (above) to taste

1 cup (235 ml) Cheezy Sauce (page 183)

To make the spiced ketchup: Combine all the ingredients in a small pot and cook over medium heat. Stir until the sauce begins to boil, about 7 minutes. Remove the pot from the heat. Let cool. Store in an air-tight container (or squeezy bottle) in the refrigerator. Keeps for at least 1 month.

To make the sandwiches: Start by combining water, soy sauce, steak sauce, garlic powder, onion powder, and pepper in a medium-size pot. Bring to a simmer. Add in the thinly sliced seitan and simmer for about 5 minutes. You aren't cooking it here, just getting it hot and infusing it with lots of juicy flavor. Turn off the heat.

Prepare the buns by spreading each half with a teaspoon of butter. Heat a pan with a lid over medium heat. Place buns butter side down and cover. (This will soften the tops of the buns as they get nice and toasty on the buttered side.) Cook until buns are golden brown.

Slather (or squirt, if you use a squeezy bottle like I do) a generous amount of spiced ketchup on the bottoms of the buns. Using tongs, remove slices of seitan from the hot broth and shake off excess liquid. Layer on ½ pound (227 g) on top of the spiced ketchup. Ladle ¼ cup (60 ml) of Cheezy Sauce on top of the seitan and add the top of the bun.

Serve immediately.

YIELD: JUST OVER 1 CUP (250 ML) SPICED KETCHUP, AND 4 SANDWICHES

You Are SO Vegan!

No recipe note here, but a little background as to how this vegan copycat came to be. Maybe you've seen the open letter to vegetarians that Arby's wrote as part of an ad campaign. Then maybe you, like me, were like, "That's pretty f'd up!" Not to mention just plain stupid. (I mean, I'm up for a good joke, but this was just a dumb marketing idea.) A bunch of vegans headed to their Facebook page and took over the comments . . . but Instagram user @UnhealthyVegan (a.k.a. André Avena) took it next level and started an entire book. A picture book, to be exact. Vegans united to post a vegan version of an Arby's menu item, but better. Better for the animals. Better for the planet. Better for our health. André was there to make sure Arby's knew that #WeMadeArbysBetter. (Go check it out!)

GREEN CASTLE SLIDERS

Nut Free

With the introduction of not one, but two different vegan options at White Castle (first the Veggie Slider and now the Impossible Burger Slider!), not only can you get your fix at home with this recipe, but you can actually get the real thing if you have a White Castle in your neck of the woods! These are really cool, because after you make them, you can just refrigerate the logs and slice them up whenever you want a little burger. You can get at least twenty sliders from this recipe. Serve them like the original sliders with diced white onion and a slice of pickle on a soft white bun. I like to use tear-apart dinner rolls, as they are the perfect size and nice and soft.

2 cups (288 g) vital wheat gluten flour

2 cups (240 g) whole wheat pastry flour

½ cup (60 g) nutritional yeast

1 tablespoon (6 g) ground black pepper

1 tablespoon (8 g) onion powder

1 tablespoon (8 g) garlic powder

1 tablespoon (7 g) paprika

1 tablespoon (8 g) cayenne pepper

1½ cups (355 ml) water

⅔ cup (160 ml) olive oil

⅔ cup (160 ml) tamari or soy sauce

⅓ cup (94 g) ketchup

YIELD: 20 SLIDERS

Preheat the oven to 350°F (180°C, or gas mark 4).

In a large bowl, combine the flours, nutritional yeast, black pepper, onion powder, garlic powder, paprika, and cayenne.

In a separate bowl, combine the water, oil, tamari, and ketchup.

Add the wet ingredients to the dry and incorporate well. Using your hands, knead the dough for several minutes. Let sit for about 10 minutes.

Divide the dough into 2 equal pieces.

Maneuver the wet mushy mass into a log shape in the center of a large piece of aluminum foil. Roll it tightly into a log, about 2 inches (5 cm) in diameter, twisting the ends nice and tight. Repeat with the other piece.

Place both logs in the oven, directly on the racks, and bake for 90 minutes.

Remove and let cool, and then unwrap.

Slice into pieces about ½ inch (1.3 cm) thick and serve.

You Are SO Vegan!

Make it a Breakfast Waffle Slider by sandwiching the slider between 2 mini vegan waffles and adding a mini Fried Egg Tofu Burger (page 20) and a slice of your favorite American-style vegan cheese.

CRUNCH WRAP SUPREME BURGER

When Taco Bell first introduced the Crunch Wrap Supreme in 2005, it was literally a month after I went vegan (insert sad face emoji here) so I never had the chance to try the real thing. Lauded as the ultimate in portability, this bad boy was a giant flour tortilla filled with seasoned ground beef and topped with nacho cheese sauce wrapped around a crispy fried corn tortilla, which was topped with sour cream, lettuce, and tomato. Here, we are subbing the meat for a burger, for added portability.

4 extra large burrito- size flour tortillas

1 recipe Ortega Burgers (page 122)

1 cup (235 ml) Nacho Cheesy Sauce (page 188)

4 corn tortillas (4-inch [10-cm]), fried or baked until crispy

1 cup (36 g) shredded green leaf lettuce

½ cup (126 g) diced tomato

½ cup (120 g) nondairy sour cream, store-bought or homemade (page 198)

YIELD: 4 BURGERS

Start by warming your tortilla slightly in a dry pan, to make it soft and pliable.

Place a burger patty in the center of the tortilla and top with ¼ cup (60 ml) Nacho Cheesy Sauce. Place a crispy corn tortilla on top of the sauce. Add ¼ cup (9 g) shredded lettuce and 2 tablespoons (42 g) diced tomato on top of the corn tortilla. Drizzle on 2 tablespoons (30 g) sour cream.

Preheat a dry pan over medium-high heat.

The hardest part (which is still pretty easy!) is to wrap the tortilla around the whole thing! Start by folding the closest edge of the tortilla up and over the top, holding it in place with one hand. Using your free hand, begin folding small sections up over the top and holding in place with your hand, overlapping each section slightly as you work your way around. I usually make six folds to complete. Carefully transfer to a dry frying pan, folded side down and press with a spatula to toast and seal. Flip and toast flat side. Repeat with remaining burgers.

You Are SO Vegan!

Skip this entire recipe and order up a vegan version of the Crunchwrap Supreme at your local Taco Bell! That's right! Just sub in beans for the meat and say no to the nacho cheese sauce and sour cream. Add guacamole—because guacamole—and you have your own vegan version in the comfort of your driver's seat!

MAC AND CHEESE BURGER

While technically not fast food, casual chains like Red Robin, TGI Fridays, and The Cheesecake Factory have all jumped on the Mac and Cheese Burger train of late. My version is in no way less decadent.

FOR THE MAC AND CHEESE:

1 pound (454 g) elbow macaroni, prepared in lightly salted water

½ cup (120 g) nondairy sour cream, store-bought or homemade (page 198)

½ cup (112 g) nondairy butter

½ cup (60 g) nutritional yeast

2 tablespoons (36 g) white miso

2 teaspoons paprika

2 teaspoons garlic powder

1 teaspoon ground mustard

Salt and pepper, to taste

FOR THE BURGERS:

4 buns of choice (I like the Agave Wheat Buns on page 213 for this one)

4 Noochy Burgers (page 46), prepared

Mac and Cheese (above)

½ cup (113 g) Aioli Dipping Sauce (page 195)

YIELD: 4 BURGERS

To make the mac and cheese: Prepare the pasta. Drain and return to the pot. Throw in all of the remaining ingredients and mix together well. Keep warm until ready to use.

To make the burgers: Get those buns nice and toasty before assembling. The toasty-ness will help prevent the bun from getting soggy under all this creamy goodness before assembling.

Layer in the following order: Bottom bun; spread with 2 tablespoons (30 g) aioli, burger patty; add, a generous pile of mac and cheese; add the, top bun; spread with 2 more tablespoons (30 g) aioli.

Serve with remaining mac and cheese on the side or save that dish for later because this burger is gonna fill you up!

You Are SO Vegan!

While definitely delving into the ridiculous category, (I mean donut-and-ramen buns are a thing now, amirite?) you can go wild and use the Savory Noodle Kugle Burger (page 83) as the buns for this one. Seriously. If you do it, please take a pic and tag me on Instagram (@jonimarienewman). Otherwise, it didn't happen.

FAST FOOD AND VEGANISM

Fast food is both loved and hated. And vegans are no different. The rapid growth of plant-based diets and veganism (In 2018 sales of plant-based foods grew over 20%, out-pacing the 2% increase in overall food sales - according to a Plant Based Foods Association funded study) and the availability of vegan options at mainstream grocery stores, fast-casual chain restaurants, and even the corner drive-thru has created quite a debate in the vegan community.

Is buying the vegan burger at Carl's Jr. just giving more money to a company that bases its business on charbroiled cow flesh? Are fast food joints only adding vegan options to their menus to profit off of the "trend"? Do these places use the same cooking equipment for their meat and vegan options? Isn't fast food unhealthy?

Well, to be frank, the answer to all of the above questions is YES.

But, here's the thing, I've personally spoken to many pre-vegans who have opted for the vegan option because they are trying to cut back on their meat consumption. Isn't that the goal? To replace meat with a more compassionate option? These companies are HUGE and wouldn't add a menu item unless they were sure it was going to help their bottom line. They, along with food giants such as Tyson, see the writing on the wall and are diversifying their portfolios, so they are not left behind when the vegan revolution becomes a reality. This. Is. A. Good. Thing.

And, newsflash, not every vegan is doing it for their health. Most vegans I know are ethical vegans who refuse to use animals for their pleasure and know that plant-based foods are better for the environment, not personal purists who worry much about shared equipment. I fall into this category. If my dollar is spent on a vegan option, I am not going to freak out that it was cooked on the same grill as animal flesh. Is it ideal? Nope. But, I'll take the vegan burger over the side salad without dressing anyday.

Can we all agree that having these options on the menu is a step in the right direction? Seeing vegan options on the menu at national chains, and in neighborhoods and parts of the country that have little to no vegan choices when dining out, will normalize the term vegan and, in the very least, show folks that plant-based options can be as delicious (and profitable!) as their cruel, animal-based counterparts.

Is rampant consumerism the best path to a better future? Maybe not. But the more available, more convenient, and more affordable plant-based options become, the easier it is for everyday people to make more ethical decisions when choosing how to spend their hard-earned dollar. Regardless of where you stand on the issue, let's do better, as vegans, to stop the food shaming, and celebrate the expansive growth that veganism has been, and continues to enjoy.

Chapter 11

LOOSE "MEAT" SANDWICHES

Sliced, stacked, piled high, or scooped, these messy, meaty filled sammies might not be patties, but they sure are tasty!

DELI-STYLE NO-TUNA MELT

Gluten-Free

Nut Free

This tastes like tuna salad. Really! Use this recipe as a guideline, but feel free to add or take out any ingredients you feel should be in your "tuna" melt. This is perfect grilled between 2 slices of sourdough, with Dijon mustard, 2 slices of Roma tomato, and a slice of vegan cheese, as shown here.

8 ounces (227 g) plain soy tempeh, crumbled into tiny pieces

¼ cup (60 g) sweet pickle relish

½ cup (112 g) vegan mayonnaise, store-bought or homemade (page 197)

½ cup (80 g) diced red onion

¼ teaspoon dill

Salt and pepper, to taste

———————

YIELD: ENOUGH FOR 4 TO 6 SANDWICHES

Mix together all the ingredients in a bowl. Refrigerate until ready to use. You can use this on a sandwich or on a bed of greens for a no-tuna salad.

If making a melt, preheat a cast-iron skillet or pan over high heat.

To get a truly fabulous melt, use mayo instead of butter on your bread when grilling. Use a pan with a lid to get the cheese nice and melty before the bread burns. Don't have a pan with a lid? You can invert a metal bowl to get the same effect!

To get the best browning without too much added fat and calories, spray the pan with nonstick spray, then cook until browned, applying pressure from the top with a spatula, then spray the top with cooking spray, flip, and apply pressure until browned.

You Are SO Vegan!

Some people find that steaming the tempeh prior to crumbling it mellows the flavor a bit. If you are the type that is tempeh hesitant or just plain old don't like tempeh, don't give up on this salad. Cut the tempeh block in half and steam in or over simmering water for 20 minutes. Some folks even say that this helps make the tempeh more digestible.

SLOPPY JONIS
(SEE WHAT I DID THERE?)

Gluten-Free

Nut Free

Weeknight meals made easy! Thanks to the use of the versatile TVP and everybody's favorite condiment . . . KETCHUP! You can replace the ketchup with barbecue sauce for a tangy twist. Either way, serve it up on a Soft White Bun (page 206).

1 cup (96 g) TVP granules

1 cup (235 ml) veggie broth (no-beef flavored vegetable broth works best here, but any will do)

¼ cup (60 ml) vegetable oil

¼ cup (40 g) finely diced onion

¼ cup (40 g) finely diced green bell pepper

4 cloves garlic, minced

1 tablespoon (15 g) prepared yellow mustard

¾ cup (204 g) ketchup

1 tablespoon (15 g) steak sauce

1 tablespoon (14 g) packed brown sugar

Salt and pepper, to taste

YIELD: 4 SERVINGS

Reconstitute TVP by mixing together with veggie broth in a microwave safe dish, covering tightly with plastic wrap and microwave on high for 5 to 6 minutes. Alternatively, you can bring the broth to a boil, pour over the TVP, mix, cover, and let sit for 10 minutes.

In a frying pan, preheat oil over medium-high heat.

Add onions and bell pepper. Sauté about 3 minutes. Add in garlic and continue to sauté for about 2 more minutes.

Reduce heat to low, add in reconstituted TVP, mustard, ketchup, steak sauce, and brown sugar.

Stir to coat, and heat through.

Add salt and pepper to taste.

You Are SO Vegan!

Replace the TVP with prepared green lentils for a more whole foods approach.

CHICKEN SALAD SAMMY

Gluten-Free

No-Sugar Added

Although there is a lot of tofu in this salad, the real star is the crunch from all the fresh, raw veggies. Serve on a sandwich, in a wrap, or on a bed of greens, or eat it with a fork right out of the bowl!

12 ounces (340 g) extra-firm tofu, drained and pressed

2 tablespoons (30 ml) olive oil

4 to 6 cloves garlic, minced

½ cup (54 g) shredded carrot

1 red onion, chopped

2 stalks celery, chopped

½ cup (60 g) walnut pieces

1 cup (150 g) grapes (green or red, or even raisins), halved

1 cup (224 g) vegan mayonnaise, store-bought or homemade (page 197)

Salt and pepper

YIELD: ENOUGH FOR 4 TO 6 SANDWICHES

Chop up the tofu into tiny, tiny, tiny pieces.

Heat the olive oil in a skillet over medium-high heat and add the garlic. Sauté for a minute. Add the tofu and sauté until golden, 7 to 10 minutes. Remove from the heat and let cool.

Add carrot, onion, celery, walnuts, grapes, mayonnaise, and salt and pepper to taste. Stir to combine.

Chill before serving.

You Are SO Vegan!

A tip for pressing tofu: After you've drained the excess liquid from the package, place the block sandwiched between two folded dish towels. Place a heavy book or pan on top to gently press the moisture out and let sit for 30 minutes to 1 hour to completely press.

PASTRAMI STACK

Nut Free

Oh, Pastrami! You are so salty and savory and fatty and just a tad sweet and taste magnificent with a big thick smear of deli mustard and provolone on toasty sourdough. My husband and I used to travel far and wide for a giant pastrami sandwich in our pregan days, and the both of us really had a hankering for nostalgia. We set out to recreate this old favorite at home using seitan and traditional pastrami spices. It had to be juicy. It had to be tangy. It had to have that peppered crust. And it had to have that signature pink marbling. After all, we eat with our eyes first, and this had to look as authentic as possible. We wanted it to be like those artisan carving board sandwiches you see on all the food shows. You know, the ones they serve up at all the hipster gastro pubs. Except ours, well, ours had to be vegan.

FOR THE SEITAN DOUGH:

2 cups (288 g) vital wheat gluten flour

1 cup (125 g) all-purpose flour

¼ cup (55 g) tightly packed brown sugar

2 tablespoons (20 g) minced garlic

1 tablespoon (6 g) freshly cracked black pepper

1 tablespoon (11 g) ground mustard seed

1 teaspoon sea salt

1 cup (235 ml) vegan beef-flavored vegetable broth

2 tablespoons (30 ml) mild-flavored vegetable oil

Vegan red food coloring (optional)

To make the seitan dough: In a mixing bowl, add vital wheat gluten, flour, brown sugar, garlic, pepper, mustard seed, and salt. Stir to combine.

Create a well in the center and slowly add in the broth and oil. Using your hands work the liquid into the flour mixture until a sticky wet dough is formed. Knead the dough for 5 solid minutes. You can do this right in the bowl.

If you want that marbled effect (tastes the same either way!) add in a few drops of red food color and knead some more to marble the dough. Add as much or as little as you like to get the desired effect.

Allow dough to rest for 15 minutes.

While resting, preheat the oven to 350°F (180°C, or gas mark 4). Have ready a rimmed baking sheet and a large piece of foil.

To make the spice rub: Simply mix together all the ingredients in a small bowl.

Lay the piece of foil flat on the counter. Transfer the dough to the center of the foil and form into a rectangle-shape slab about 6 inches (15 cm) wide, 8 inches (20 cm) long, and 3 inches (7.5 cm) thick. This does not need to be exact.

Coat the entire surface with the spice rub, flip over, and coat the bottom with the rub.

FOR THE SPICE RUB:

¼ cup (55 g) tightly packed brown sugar

2 tablespoons (14 g) smoked paprika

2 tablespoons (12 g) ground black pepper

1 tablespoon (2 g) dried coriander

FOR THE SIMMERING BROTH:

2 cups (470 ml) vegan beef-flavored vegetable broth

2 tablespoons (30 g) spicy brown mustard

¼ cup tightly packed brown sugar

¼ cup sea salt

1 tablespoon smoked paprika

1 tablespoon minced garlic

1 bay leaf

YIELD: 2 POUNDS (908 G) PASTRAMI

Roll the slab up in the foil as tightly as possible. If you need a second piece of foil, use it. (You need to wrap it as tight as possible so the seitan does not expand while baking. You want it to remain trapped in the foil so it remains dense, not bready.)

Place on the baking sheet and bake, wrapped, for 45 minutes. After 45 minutes, carefully remove from the oven. Allow to cool for a few minutes before carefully unwrapping.

Place the partially baked slab in the center of the pan (you can line with parchment or anther piece of foil to help with cleanup, if you choose) and bake an additional 30 minutes uncovered. It should be blackened and hard to the touch when ready.

Meanwhile, to make the simmering broth: Add all broth ingredients to a pot and bring to a boil. Boil for 5 minutes to make sure all the salt and sugar has dissolved, then reduce the heat to a medium low simmer.

Remove blackened Pastrami slab from the oven and allow to cool to the touch. Using a sharp serrated knife, cut the pastrami into thin slices. As thin as you can! If you are lucky enough to have one of those deli-meat-spinning slicers, now is an amazing time to bust it out!

Place the slices into the simmering broth. Serve the pastrami straight from the broth. If you are planning to serve it later, make sure to store the pastrami in the broth to keep it moist and juicy.

You Are SO Vegan!

This pastrami also makes a mean base for a Reuben. To make it a Reuben, use toasted rye instead of a bun. Slather one slice of the bread with spicy brown mustard, the other slice with Better Sauce (page 159), and don't forget a healthy dose of sauerkraut to bring it all together.

PULLED "PORK" SLIDERS

Nut Free

These tasty little plant-based pork sliders will fool the best of them. But why try to fool them?

Oil, for frying

3 (20 ounce [565 g] each) cans young green jackfruit in brine or water, drained, rinsed, and patted dry

3½ cups (825 ml) Quick & Simple BBQ Sauce (page 190), or your favorite BBQ Sauce

1 medium yellow onion, julienne cut

12 soft dinner rolls (If you can find vegan Hawaiian sweet rolls, use those!)

1 recipe Creamy BBQ Coleslaw (page 227), prepared

YIELD: 12 SLIDERS

Heat enough oil to coat the bottom of your frying pan or skillet over medium-high heat.

Add the jackfruit chunks in a single layer and fry until almost completely blackened. This can take up to 10 minutes. Flip and repeat on the other side.

Remove from heat and allow to cool enough to handle.

Using the tines of a fork, shred the jackfruit until it resembles, well, shredded pork.

Mix the shredded jackfruit, barbecue sauce, and onion together and add to your slow cooker. Cook on medium for 3 hours. Alternatively, use a pot with a tight-fitting lid and simmer, covered, on medium-low heat for 90 minutes, returning every so often to stir.

Split the dinner rolls in half. Pile on equal parts coleslaw and jackfruit and serve.

You Are SO Vegan!

For a No-Oil Added option, bake the jackfruit, uncovered, in a single layer, for 45 minutes at 375°F (190°C, or gas mark 5), flipping halfway through before shredding.

PHILLY CHEESESTEAK

No-Sugar Added

Serve this classic sandwich on game night to satisfy those sporty cravings.

FOR CHEEZY SAUCE:

2 cups (470 ml) soy creamer

½ cup (60 g) nutritional yeast

½ cup (65 g) raw cashews

1 tablespoon (16 g) tahini

2 tablespoons (36 g) white miso

2 tablespoons (16 g) cornstarch

1 tablespoon (8 g) onion powder

1 tablespoon (8 g) garlic powder

1 tablespoon (8 g) ground mustard

FOR SANDWICHES:

Vegetable oil, for frying

2 large white onions, sliced or diced

2 red, green, or yellow bell peppers, sliced into thin strips or diced

½ recipe Green Castle Sliders (page 170), prepared but not sliced

Salt and pepper

4 French rolls

YIELD: 2½ CUPS (588 ML) CHEEZY SAUCE AND ENOUGH FILLING TO MAKE 4 SANDWICHES

To make the cheezy sauce: Place all the ingredients in a blender or food processor and process until smooth. Place in a saucepan. Heat over low heat until it thickens, constantly stirring so it doesn't get clumpy or scorch.

To make the sandwiches: Slice the slider dough into strips about 1 inch (2.5 cm) wide and 4 to 6 inches (10 to 15 cm) long.

In a large frying pan, preheat about 3 tablespoons (45 ml) of oil, adding more later as you continue cooking. Sauté some of the onions, some of the peppers, and some of the slider strips, in amounts you like for your sammies. Season with salt and pepper. Pile high onto the French rolls and drizzle with the cheezy sauce.

You Are SO Vegan!

Skip the seitan for a more veggie-based Sammy by subbing portobello strips for the slider strips in this recipe. Use gluten-free rolls, and this baby will be gluten-free, too!

TOFU EGG SALAD SAMMY

Gluten-Free

No-Sugar Added

I used to love the egg salad sandwiches my mom made for us. They were pretty plain. No onions, no pickles, no capers. Just eggs, mayo, and a smidge of mustard. Well, I'm all grown up now, with grown-up taste buds. This is my take on my childhood favorite. I like to cut my tofu into tiny cubes for this recipe, because I like the toothier feel to the cubes. Crumble it to make it more "yolky." Cube it to make it more "eggy."

2 tablespoons (30 ml) olive oil

1 cup (160 g) diced white or yellow onion

4 cloves garlic, minced

12 ounces (340 g) extra-firm tofu, drained, pressed, and cubed

¼ cup (30 g) nutritional yeast

¼ teaspoon turmeric

½ teaspoon ground mustard

⅛ teaspoon dill

⅛ teaspoon paprika

½ cup (112 g) vegan mayonnaise, store-bought or homemade (page 197)

1 tablespoon (15 g) yellow mustard

½ teaspoon Kala Namak (black salt)

Pepper

In a skillet, heat the oil over medium-high heat and sauté the onion and garlic until fragrant, 3 to 4 minutes.

Add the tofu and sauté for 10 to 12 minutes, or until golden.

Lower the heat and add the nutritional yeast, turmeric, ground mustard, dill, and paprika.

Fold until well coated, then remove from the heat and let cool.

Add the mayonnaise, mustard, and Kala Namak. Mix well. Add pepper to taste.

Keep refrigerated until ready to serve.

YIELD: ENOUGH FOR 8 WRAPS OR SANDWICHES

You Are SO Vegan!

I didn't make this as a low-fat recipe, because, made as written, it tastes soooo good! But, if you are worried about the added fat, you can reduce the amount of oil in the pan, or eliminate it altogether and use an olive oil cooking spray instead. For the mayo, you could use plain soy yogurt instead, but it will be tangier.

Chapter 12

FIXIN'S

Toppings, sauces, dips, and such, to give your burger the perfect touch.

NACHO CHEESY SAUCE

Perfect to top the Jalapeño Cornbread Burger (page 85) but also great on tortilla chips, tacos, burritos, and even chili.

No-Sugar Added   No-Oil Added

2 cups (470 ml) plain soy creamer

½ cup (60 g) nutritional yeast

½ cup (65 g) raw cashews

1 tablespoon (16 g) tahini

2 tablespoons (36 g) white miso

2 tablespoons (16 g) cornstarch

1 tablespoon (8 g) onion powder

1 tablespoon (8 g) garlic powder

1 tablespoon (8 g) ground mustard

1 teaspoon ground cumin

1 teaspoon hot sauce, or more to taste

2 to 4 slices jarred or canned jalapeños

1 tablespoon (15 ml) juice from jar of jalapeños

YIELD: 2½ CUPS (590 G)

Place all the ingredients in a blender or food processor and process until smooth.

Place in a saucepan. Heat over low heat until it thickens, stirring constantly so it doesn't get clumpy or scorch. Store in an airtight container in the refrigerator until ready to use.

TANGY TAHINI SAUCE

Gluten-Free Nut Free No-Sugar Added

This tangy sauce works so well as a spread for many of the burgers in this book, including the Super Quinoa Burger (page 95) and The Trifecta Burger (page 69). It is also delicious as a salad dressing or dip for veggies.

1 container (6 ounces, [170 g]) plain soy yogurt

3 tablespoons (48 g) tahini

2 tablespoons (30 ml) sesame oil

1 tablespoon (15 ml) lemon juice

½ teaspoon dill

½ teaspoon paprika

Salt and pepper

YIELD: 1 CUP (240 G)

Place all the ingredients in a blender and blend until smooth, or whisk together very well.

Store in an airtight container in the refrigerator until ready to use.

QUICK & SIMPLE BBQ SAUCE

It takes longer to drive to the store and buy a bottle than it does to simmer up your own sweet and sassy barbecue sauce!

Nut Free

1 tablespoon (15 ml) olive oil

1 yellow onion, finely diced

16 ounces (454 g) tomato sauce

1 teaspoon onion powder

1 teaspoon garlic powder

2 tablespoons (30 ml) apple cider vinegar

2 tablespoons (44 g) molasses

½ teaspoon freshly ground black pepper

2 tablespoons (40 g) grape jelly

2 tablespoons (30 ml) soy sauce

¼ teaspoon liquid smoke (optional)

YIELD: 3 CUPS (705 ML)

Heat the oil in a skillet and sauté the onion until fragrant and translucent, 5 to 7 minutes. Add the tomato sauce, onion powder, garlic powder, vinegar, molasses, pepper, jelly, and soy sauce and bring to a simmer. Simmer over low heat, uncovered, for about 10 minutes, stirring occasionally. Remove from the heat. Stir in the liquid smoke, if using. If you don't like chunks of onion in your barbecue sauce, let cool and run through a blender or food processor until smooth.

STRAWBERRY BBQ SAUCE

Gluten-Free *Nut Free* *Soy-Free*

Sweet, smoky, tangy, and a little bit of heat makes this unique barbecue sauce the perfect addition to your sauce repertoire!

2 tablespoons (30 ml) vegetable oil

½ cup (80 g) diced yellow onion

½ cup (80 g) diced red onion

2 tablespoons (17 g) minced garlic

1 pound (454 g) fresh strawberries, stems removed and cut into quarters

¼ teaspoon salt

¼ teaspoon black pepper

1 can (15 ounces [425 g]) diced tomatoes in juice

8 ounces (227 g) tomato sauce

½ cup (110 g) tightly packed brown sugar

¼ to ½ teaspoon chipotle powder, add more or less to taste

¼ teaspoon red chili flakes, add more or less to taste

YIELD: 3 CUPS (705 ML)

In a pot, heat oil over medium-high heat. Add yellow and red onions and sauté for 3 minutes. Add garlic and sauté an additional 3 minutes, or until fragrant and translucent. Add in strawberries, salt, and pepper. Continue to cook for an additional 5 minutes, stirring often.

Stir in diced tomatoes, tomato sauce, brown sugar, chipotle powder, and chili flakes. Bring to a boil, reduce to a simmer and simmer uncovered for 30 minutes, returning to stir a few times. Remove from heat. Using an immersion blender (or carefully transfer to a tabletop blender) blend smooth, if desired.

Store in an airtight container in the refrigerator for up to 2 weeks.

INDIAN-SPICED MAYO

Here's another aioli-type spread that tastes great on the Middle Eastern inspired burgers throughout this book.

Gluten-Free

1 cup (225 g) vegan mayonnaise, store-bought or homemade (page 197)

1 tablespoon (8 g) garam masala

Pinch of paprika

Pinch of turmeric

Salt and pepper, to taste

Combine all the ingredients in an airtight container and keep refrigerated until ready to use.

YIELD: 1 CUP (225 G)

CHIPOTLE DIPPING SAUCE

I especially like the way the spiciness of this sauce plays off the sweetness of the Chipotle Sweet Potato Burger (page 99) and Baked Sweet Potato Fries (page 216). This sauce also works well as a spread for sandwiches, or even on the bun under your Edamame Burger (page 144).

Gluten-Free

1 cup (240 g) nondairy sour cream, store-bought or homemade (page 198)

½ teaspoon chipotle powder

½ teaspoon garlic powder

¼ teaspoon dillweed

Salt and pepper, to taste

Place all the ingredients in a bowl and mix well.

Keep refrigerated until ready to use. The longer you refrigerate it, the more the chipotle flavor will develop.

YIELD: 1 CUP (240 G)

SIMPLE PESTO

I usually double this recipe, using half for the Sun-Dried Tomato and Artichoke Burger (page 107) or Garlic, Mushroom, and Onion Seitanic Stuffer (page 116) and reserving the other half to spread on a toasted bun or throw on some pasta later.

14 large fresh basil leaves

2 or 3 cloves garlic

½ teaspoon coarse sea salt

1 tablespoon (8 g) toasted pine nuts

1 tablespoon (8 g) raw walnut pieces

1 tablespoon (8 g) nutritional yeast

3 tablespoons (45 ml) olive oil

In a food processor, combine the basil, garlic, salt, pine nuts, walnuts, and nutritional yeast and process until a purée is formed.

Drizzle in the oil and pulse a few more times to combine.

YIELD: ½ CUP (130 G)

SUN-DRIED TOMATO AIOLI

This works well on almost any of the burgers in this book, and as a sandwich or bagel spread.

2 cloves garlic

¼ cup (28 g) sun-dried tomatoes packed in oil

¼ teaspoon paprika

¼ cup (30 g) pine nuts

¾ cup (168 g) vegan mayonnaise, store-bought or homemade (page 197)

Salt and pepper

In a food processor, combine the garlic, tomatoes, and paprika and process until smooth. Transfer to a bowl.

Add the pine nuts, mayonnaise, and salt and pepper to taste. Stir to combine.

Store in an airtight container, in the fridge, until ready to use.

YIELD: JUST OVER 1 CUP (250 G)

GARLIC ARTICHOKE SPREAD

This works well as a burger or sandwich spread and as a dip for crackers and veggies. It is especially yummy on the Baba Ghanoush Burger (page 152).

---

2 tablespoons (30 ml) plus ¼ cup (60 ml) olive oil, divided

1 yellow onion, chopped

2 tablespoons (30 g) minced garlic

½ teaspoon ground cumin

Pinch of salt and freshly cracked pepper

1 can (14 ounces [392 g]) artichoke hearts, drained and roughly chopped

½ cup (60 g) pine nuts (optional)

Preheat the 2 tablespoons (30 ml) oil over medium-high heat in a flat-bottomed skillet.

Add the onion, garlic, cumin, salt, and pepper. Sauté until translucent and fragrant and the edges of the onions just start to turn brown, 5 to 7 minutes.

Transfer to a blender or food processor (I prefer a blender for this), add the artichoke hearts and remaining ¼ cup (60 ml) oil, and blend until smooth.

Transfer to a bowl and mix in the pine nuts.

YIELD: JUST UNDER 3 CUPS (685 G)

CHUNKY MARINARA

This sauce is great for dipping Fried Zucchini (page 217), on pasta, and on the Zucchini Mushroom Burgers (page 110).

---

28 ounces (795 g) diced tomatoes with juice, no salt added

8 ounces (227 g) tomato sauce

6 ounces (170 g) tomato paste

1 tablespoon (2 g) dried basil

1 tablespoon (12 g) sugar

1 tablespoon (22 g) molasses

2 tablespoons (30 ml) olive oil

6 cloves garlic, minced

1 yellow onion, finely diced

Place the tomatoes, sauce, paste, basil, sugar, and molasses in a large stockpot. Bring to a simmer over medium-low heat.

Meanwhile, in a skillet, heat the olive oil and sauté the garlic and onion until the garlic is fragrant and the onion is translucent, about 10 minutes.

Add the garlic and onion to the pot. Cover and continue to simmer for 20 minutes.

Uncover and simmer for 10 minutes.

YIELD: JUST UNDER 4 CUPS (980 G)

AIOLI DIPPING SAUCE

This basic aioli can be your inspiration to never again be tempted to use plain old mayo—unless, of course, you love plain old mayo (like I do!).

⅔ cup (150 g) vegan mayonnaise, store-bought or homemade (page 197)

⅓ cup (80 g) nondairy sour cream, store-bought or homemade (page 198)

2 tablespoons (30 ml) extra-virgin olive oil

1½ tablespoons (23 ml) fresh lemon juice

3 tablespoons (9 g) chopped fresh basil

2 tablespoons (12 g) chopped fresh chives

1 tablespoon (15 g) minced garlic

1 tablespoon (8 g) lemon zest

½ teaspoon sea salt

½ teaspoon freshly cracked pepper

In small bowl, stir together the mayonnaise, sour cream, olive oil, and lemon juice.

Stir in the basil, chives, garlic, lemon zest, salt, and pepper.

Cover and refrigerate for at least 30 minutes, or until ready to use.

YIELD: 1½ CUPS (338 G)

CREAMY BALSAMIC DRESSING

This dressing (mentioned on the Scarborough Fair Tofu Burger on page 72) is my answer to a creamy garlic dressing that is served at one of my favorite Italian restaurants. Unfortunately for me, that dressing contains beef consommé and, therefore, is not vegan.

12 ounces (340 g) extra-firm tofu, drained but not pressed

½ cup (120 ml) olive oil

¼ cup (60 ml) balsamic vinegar

1 tablespoon (8 g) garlic powder

1 tablespoon (8 g) onion powder

Salt and pepper, to taste

Place all the ingredients in a blender and process until smooth.

Keep refrigerated in an airtight container until ready to use. Lasts about 1 week.

YIELD: 1½ CUPS (375 G)

VEGAN MAYONNAISE TWO WAYS

EASY TOFU CASHEW MAYO

7 ounces (195 g) extra-firm tofu, drained and pressed

¼ cup (35 g) raw cashews, ground into a very fine powder

1 tablespoon (15 ml) lemon juice

1 tablespoon (12 g) raw sugar or (21 g) agave nectar

1½ teaspoons brown or Dijon mustard

1 teaspoon apple cider or rice wine vinegar

½ teaspoon sea salt

6 tablespoons (90 ml) canola oil

Place the tofu, cashews, lemon juice, sugar, mustard, vinegar, and salt in a blender or food processor and process until smooth.

Slowly drizzle in the oil and pulse until you get the consistency that you like.

Store in an airtight container in the refrigerator for up to 2 weeks.

YIELD: ALMOST 2 CUPS (450 G)

AQUAFABA MAYO

¼ cup (60 ml) liquid from a can of garbanzo beans (a.k.a. aquafaba), room temperature

2 teaspoons lemon juice, lime juice, or apple cider vinegar (your choice)

½ teaspoon dried ground mustard seed

¼ teaspoon salt

¼ teaspoon sugar*

¾ cup (180 ml) mild-flavored vegetable oil

*If you prefer to use a liquid sweetener, such as agave or date syrup, do not add until after the mayo has emulsified and thickened. Simply stir it in afterward.

Add the aquafaba, juice or vinegar, mustard seed, salt, and sugar* to the cup of your immersion blender. If your immersion blender did not come with a cup, a wide-mouthed glass jar will work. Make sure to use a tall, slender container for this. A regular bowl will not work. Blend until white and foamy, about 15 seconds.

Slowly drizzle in oil in a very thin stream, a small amount at a time, while constantly blending. Allow the oil to completely incorporate before adding more. DO NOT STOP THE BLENDER DURING THE ENTIRE PROCESS! Continue to add oil until it is all incorporated. This process should take up to 5 full minutes. Be patient. Be *very, very* patient. Upon adding the last of the oil, it should be thick and silky . . . just like mayo. Keep refrigerated in an airtight container until ready to use. Should last up to 2 weeks. Use as is as mayo or add additional seasonings to make a variety of aiolis, spreads, and sauces.

YIELD: 1 CUP (235 ML)

NONDAIRY SOUR CREAM

Although nondairy versions of traditionally dairy products are becoming more readily available, you might occasionally need to whip up a delicious batch of your own, especially if you are making the Three Bean Chili Burger on page 63 or the Denver Omelet Burger on page 19 (where this recipe is pictured).

7 ounces (195 g) extra-firm tofu, drained well and pressed

¼ cup (28 g) raw cashews, ground into a fine powder

1 tablespoon (15 ml) white rice vinegar

1 tablespoon (15 ml) lemon or lime juice

1 tablespoon (18 g) white miso

1 tablespoon (15 ml) mild-flavored vegetable oil

Place all the ingredients in a blender or food processor and process until very, very smooth and creamy. Keep refrigerated in an airtight container until ready to use. Should last up to 1 week.

YIELD: ABOUT 1½ CUPS (345 G)

SWEET MUSTARD SAUCE

This innocent sauce offers a bit of sweet relief when slathered onto some of the more spicy burgers in this book. It is especially tasty on the Jalapeño Cheddar Burger (page 126).

½ cup (120 g) vegan mayonnaise, store-bought or homemade (page 197)

2 tablespoons (42 g) agave nectar

2 tablespoons (30 g) Dijon mustard

1 tablespoon (6 g) finely diced chives

Salt and pepper

Whisk together all the ingredients.

Store in an airtight container in the refrigerator until ready to use.

YIELD: ¾ CUP (190 G)

TZATZIKI SAUCE

Gluten-Free *Nut Free* *No-Sugar Added*

*Fresh and tangy, this sauce works well with falafel, in a pita sandwich,
or as a dip for warm pita triangles or flatbread. It is also great on
Lizzy's Lentil Burger on page 58.*

12 ounces (340 g) unsweetened plain soy or other nondairy yogurt

1½ cups (200 g) seeded and finely diced cucumber

1 tablespoon (3 g) fresh dill

1 tablespoon (15 g) minced garlic

1 tablespoon (15 ml) lemon juice

1 tablespoon (15 ml) olive oil

Salt and pepper

Strain the excess liquid from the yogurt by pouring the yogurt into the center of several folded layers of cheesecloth, tying it off, and suspending it over a bowl. I use the handle of a wooden spoon to tie my cheesecloth to and then rest each end of the spoon over the edge of a mixing bowl. Let sit for a few hours.

In a bowl, combine the strained yogurt, cucumber, dill, garlic, lemon juice, oil, and salt and pepper to taste.

Keep refrigerated in an airtight container until ready to use. This should keep for about 1 week.

YIELD: JUST OVER 2 CUPS (480 G)

THAI PEANUT SAUCE

No-Sugar Added

*A very simple sauce that is great for dipping, pouring, and serving over pasta, and
especially good slathered all over the Thai-Inspired Black Bean Tofu and Potato
Patties on page 146. Use gluten-free tamari to make this gluten-free.*

½ cup (128 g) peanut butter

½ cup (120 ml) peanut oil

⅓ cup (33 g) chopped scallion

2 tablespoons (30 ml) soy sauce or tamari

1 teaspoon dried red pepper flakes

Combine the peanut butter, oil, scallion, soy sauce, and red pepper flakes in a blender and purée until smooth.

YIELD: JUST OVER 1 CUP (240 G)

MOM'S MANGO SALSA

My mom rocks. She always makes sure that there is enough for me to eat when I visit. This is her famous mango salsa. I could live on this stuff alone while I'm at her house.

1 mango, peeled, seeded, and diced

½ cup (8 g) finely chopped fresh cilantro

½ cup (80 g) finely diced red onion

1 teaspoon garlic powder

½ teaspoon salt, or more to taste

½ teaspoon black pepper

1 serrano chile, seeded, cored, and finely diced

In a bowl, combine all the ingredients and refrigerate overnight to enhance the flavor.

Serve with tortilla chips, or pile on top of some of the spicier burgers for a nice contrast in flavor and texture.

YIELD: ABOUT 1½ CUPS (375 G)

CREAMY SESAME SRIRACHA SAUCE

A.K.A. Spicy Sushi Sauce, this salmon-colored sauce is one of my absolute favorite sauces. To quote that sassy old lady from the Frank's Hot Sauce commercials, "I put that s#@! on everything!"

12 ounces (340 g) soft silken tofu

¾ cup (180 ml) mild- flavored vegetable oil

¼ cup (60 ml) sesame oil

3 tablespoons (45 ml) sriracha sauce

2 tablespoons (30 ml) rice vinegar

1 tablespoon (10 g) minced garlic

½ teaspoon ground mustard seed

½ teaspoon salt

Add all ingredients to a blender and blend until silky smooth. Keep stored in an airtight container in the refrigerator. This will keep for at least 2 weeks.

YIELD: ABOUT 2 CUPS (470 ML)

TACO SEASONING

Nut Free Gluten-Free Soy-Free No-Oil Added

Sure, it's easy to just buy a pack of Taco Seasoning at the store, but double check the ingredients to make sure it doesn't have any whey. Store-bought varieties also often contain additional ingredients such as anticaking agents and preservatives. To avoid this, you can make your own by mixing together the following ingredients and storing it in an airtight container.

1 tablespoon (8 g) garlic powder

1 tablespoon (8 g) onion powder

1 tablespoon (13 g) sugar

1 tablespoon (7 g) ground cumin

1 tablespoon (7 g) paprika

2 tablespoons (16 g) chili powder

1½ teaspoons salt

Place all the ingredients in a small airtight container and shake vigorously. Two tablespoons (16 g) of this mix roughly equals one packet of store-bought taco seasoning.

YIELD: ½ CUP (128 G)

IMITATION BACON BITS

No-Sugar Added Nut Free

I love a challenge, so when asked about the hydrogenated fats in imitation bacon bits, I started on a quest. Of course, buying a jar of Bac-Os is still the easiest. But, if you are a smidge adventurous, try this.

2 tablespoons (30 ml) liquid smoke

1 scant cup (225 ml) water

1 cup (96 g) TVP granules

¼ teaspoon salt

A few drops vegan red food coloring (optional)

3 tablespoons (45 ml) canola or other vegetable oil

YIELD: ABOUT 1 CUP (100 G)

To a measuring cup, add the liquid smoke, then fill with the water to get 1 cup (235 ml). In a microwave-safe dish, combine the liquid smoke mixture, TVP granules, salt, and red food coloring, if using. Cover tightly with plastic wrap and microwave for 5 to 6 minutes. Alternatively, bring the water to a boil, pour over the TVP granules mixed with the salt, mix in the liquid smoke and red food coloring, cover, and let sit for 10 minutes.

Preheat a frying pan with the oil. Add the reconstituted TVP to the pan and toss to make sure it all gets coated with oil. Panfry until desired crispness. Stir often. You don't necessarily want to brown them, but rather dry them out, about 10 minutes.

Allow to cool completely before transferring to an airtight container. Store in the refrigerator. Should last at least a week, but probably much longer.

BACON STRIPS

Nut Free

Seriously, folks, just about any vegetable can be turned into bacon. Eggplants, carrots, parsnips, mushrooms, even zucchini. What you're after is smoky, salty, fatty, and a little hint of sweet flavor. Not dead pig. So feast on veggie bacon! This marinade will work on just about any veggie with similar results.

2 tablespoons (30 ml) liquid smoke

2 tablespoons (30 ml) soy sauce or tamari

2 tablespoons (30 ml) mild-flavored vegetable oil

1 tablespoon (14 g) tightly packed brown sugar

2 teaspoons apple cider vinegar

½ teaspoon onion powder

½ teaspoon garlic powder

½ teaspoon black pepper

¼ teaspoon paprika

¼ cup (60 ml) maple syrup

1 pound (454 g) sliced vegetables, cut no more than ¼-inch (6 mm) thick

YIELD: WILL VARY DEPENDING ON AMOUNT AND TYPE OF VEGETABLES USED

Mix together all ingredients except vegetables to make a marinade.

Add sliced vegetables to a resealable plastic bag, or a shallow dish with a lid, and add enough marinade to cover completely. Allow to soak in marinade for at least 1 hour.

Preheat oven to 350°F (180°C, or gas mark 4). Line a rimmed baking sheet with parchment, and arrange marinated vegetables, along with any additional marinade, in a single layer.

Bake for 60 minutes, flipping halfway through. (Note: Some vegetables have a higher water content than others and will take a longer time to cook.)

Vegetables should have absorbed the liquid and browned. They should be crisp around the edges, but soft and chewy in the centers.

Remove from oven and allow to cool completely before storing in the refrigerator until ready to use.

If a crispier strip is desired, you can panfry on medium-high heat in a bit of oil, until desired crispness is reached.

TRADITIONAL BOILED SEITAN

This plain and simple seitan has a neutral beefy flavor and works well in recipes calling for prepared seitan.

Nut Free   No-Sugar Added   No-Oil Added

FOR BOILING BROTH:

10 cups (2.35 L) water

2 cups (470 ml) soy sauce

10 cloves garlic, chopped in half

5 whole bay leaves

3 slices (2 inches [5 cm] each) fresh ginger or 1 hand, chopped into chunks

FOR SEITAN DOUGH:

1 cup (144 g) vital wheat gluten flour

5 cups (600 g) whole wheat flour

2½ cups (588 ml) water

½ cup (32 g) chopped fresh parsley

3 scallions, whites only, finely chopped

1 teaspoon garlic powder

1 teaspoon onion powder

1 to 3 teaspoons freshly cracked pepper, to taste

YIELD: ABOUT 4 POUNDS (1816 G)

To make the broth: Combine all the broth ingredients in a large stockpot and bring to a simmer.

To make the seitan dough: In a large mixing bowl, combine the flours, then slowly add the water and form into a stiff dough. Knead the dough about 70 times. You can do it right in the bowl. Let rest for 20 minutes.

After resting, take the dough, in the bowl, to the sink and cover with water. Knead the dough until the water becomes milky, then drain off the water and repeat. Do this 10 to 12 times. By the tenth or twelfth time, the dough will feel and look loose and goopy, but the water will still be a little milky.

After the last rinse, add the parsley, scallions, garlic powder, onion powder, and pepper. Mix thoroughly by hand.

Divide the dough in half. Place 1 piece of dough in the center of a large piece of cheesecloth and roll tightly into a log shape. Tie the ends to secure. Repeat with the other piece.

Place both logs in the broth and simmer for 90 minutes.

Remove from the broth and set on a plate to cool. Unwrap. If the cheesecloth is sticking, run under some water, and it should come off easily.

You can store the seitan in the refrigerator wrapped in foil or in a plastic container. To keep it really moist, place some of the broth in the container. Will keep in the fridge for about 2 weeks, or indefinitely in the freezer.

Chapter 13

BUNS
AND
BREADS

"Cause you have to put your burger on something, right?

SOFT WHITE BUNS

Nut Free

Plain. White. Buns. You honestly can't go wrong serving any of the burgers in this book on these buns. My favorites include the All-American Burger (page 38) and the Sunday Afternoon Grillers (page 35).

---

1 cup (235 ml) plain soymilk

½ cup (120 ml) water

¼ cup (56 g) nondairy butter

4½ cups (563 g) all-purpose flour, divided

¼ ounce (7 g) quick-rise yeast

2 tablespoons (25 g) sugar

1½ teaspoons salt

Equivalent of 2 eggs*

*I have made this with flax eggs (2 tablespoons [14 g] ground flax-seeds mixed with 6 tablespoons [90 ml] water), tofu eggs (½ cup [120 ml] blended silken tofu), and Ener-G (1 tablespoon [8 g] whisked with ¼ cup [60 ml] warm water until frothy). The best buns were with the Ener-G. The others tasted fine, but didn't puff up as much.

YIELD: 8 BUNS

Line 2 baking sheets with parchment or a silicone baking mat.

In a saucepan or a microwave-safe bowl, combine the soymilk, water, and butter, and heat just until the butter is melted. In the microwave, I do this in about 1 minute. Set aside.

In a large bowl, combine half of the flour and the yeast, sugar, and salt.

Add the soymilk mixture to the flour and mix well, then add the egg replacer.

After well incorporated, mix in the remaining flour, ½ cup (62 g) at a time.

Once all of the flour has been added, and the dough begins to form into a large mass, turn it out onto a floured surface and knead for 5 to 8 minutes, until smooth and elastic.

Divide into 8 equal pieces. Roll each piece into a smooth ball. Place on the baking sheets, 4 per sheet, and press down to flatten a little (like a disc, instead of a ball). Cover loosely and let rise for 1 hour.

Preheat the oven to 400°F (200°C, or gas mark 6).

Bake for 12 to 14 minutes, or until golden on top.

Let cool for 5 minutes on the pans before transferring to racks to cool completely.

50/50 FLATBREAD

Nut Free

No-Oil Added

No-Sugar Added

These easy flatbreads make a great stand-in for pitas, and work well as a transportation device to get some of those yummy Middle Eastern–influenced burgers directly into your mouth! For another variation, add garlic and different herbs to dress up these little flatbreads.

1½ cups (180 g) whole wheat flour

1½ cups (188 g) all-purpose flour

1 tablespoon (18 g) sea salt

1¼ cups (295 ml) water

———

YIELD: 16 FLATBREADS

Combine the flours and salt in a large bowl. Slowly add the water.

Mix with your hands until you get a nice big dough ball. Knead for a few minutes.

Divide into 16 equal pieces. Press each piece flat (about the size of a small pancake).

Using a dry, nonstick pan, cook each piece, one at a time, over high heat for 1½ to 2 minutes on each side.

If you have a gas stove, turn on an extra burner. After cooking in the pan, using tongs, place the flatbread on an open flame set to low for a few seconds. It will puff up and deflate quickly. Repeat on the other side.

Stack on a plate, under a dish towel to keep warm, until all the breads are done.

CHEESY BISCUITS

Fluffy cheesy biscuits that taste great as a stand in for a bun on any of the breakfast burgers in chapter 2. Depending on the type of milk used, this recipe can be made soy- or nut-free.

1 cup (235 ml) unsweetened soy or almond milk

2 tablespoons (30 ml) lemon juice

2¼ cups (281 g) all-purpose flour

¼ cup (30 g) nutritional yeast

2 tablespoons (25 g) sugar

2 teaspoons baking powder

1 teaspoon baking soda

1½ teaspoons salt

¼ cup (60 ml) refined coconut oil, chilled until solid

½ cup (50 g) finely chopped chives, (optional)

YIELD: 8 BISCUITS

Preheat oven to 450°F (230°C, or gas mark 8). Line a baking sheet with parchment or a silicone baking mat.

Combine soymilk and lemon juice in a small bowl it will curdle and become like buttermilk.

In a large mixing bowl, combine flour, nutritional yeast, sugar, baking powder, baking soda, and salt.

Using a pastry cutter or your fingertips, work chilled coconut oil into the flour mixture until it resembles fine crumbs.

Create a well in the center and add buttermilk mixture. Mix gently and sprinkle in the chives, if using. Gently knead until it comes together, taking care not to overwork the dough.

Turn the dough out onto a well-floured surface and form the dough into a rectangle about ¾ inch (2 cm) thick. Using a cookie cutter, or an inverted pint glass, cut dough into rounds. Gently reform dough as needed to get 8 biscuits.

Arrange in a single layer, arranging so the biscuits slightly touch each other, on the baking sheet and bake for 12 to 15 minutes, or until lightly browned.

Let rest for 5 minutes before serving.

RUSTICA BUNS

Soy-Free Nut-Free

No-Sugar Added

Okay, so the name is a little goofy. But these buns really are rustic looking . . . and tasting. They are hard and dry on the outside, with nooks and crannies revealing the soft orange inside. Yummy! I enjoy these buns with all sorts of burgers, even on their own with melted, nondairy butter, but my favorite way is with the Couscous Pantry Burgers on page 91.

½ cup (60 g) chickpea flour

1½ cups (188 g) all-purpose flour, plus more for coating

¼ ounce (7 g) quick-rise yeast

½ teaspoon baking powder

½ teaspoon baking soda

¼ teaspoon salt

¼ cup (28 g) finely chopped sun-dried tomato pieces

2 cloves garlic, minced

2 tablespoons (30 ml) extra-virgin olive oil

½ cup (120 ml) water, plus more if needed

In a mixing bowl, combine the chickpea flour, 1½ cups (188 g) all-purpose flour, yeast, baking powder, baking soda, and salt.

Add the tomatoes, garlic, and olive oil, and stir to combine.

Add the ½ cup (120 ml) water and knead well. Add more water, if needed, 1 tablespoon (15 ml) at a time, until a smooth, firm dough ball is formed. Knead for a few minutes, until uniform.

Divide into 4 equal pieces. Form each piece into a ball and then flatten slightly. Pat a bit of all-purpose flour onto each bun to coat. Place on an oiled baking sheet. Cover loosely and let rise for 1 hour.

Preheat the oven to 350°F (180°C or gas mark 4).

Bake for 10 to 12 minutes, or until you see cracks forming on the tops.

YIELD: 4 BUNS

MOLASSES BUNS

Nut Free

*Sweet and soft, these buns work nicely with almost all of the burgers in the book,
especially the breakfast burgers and the Seitanic Stuffer on page 114.*

¼ ounce (7 g) active dry yeast

1 tablespoon (12 g) sugar

¼ cup (60 ml) warm water, plus more
if needed

4 cups (500 g) all-purpose flour

2 teaspoons baking soda

2 teaspoons baking powder

1 teaspoon salt

1 cup (235 ml) soy or other nondairy
milk

½ cup (112 g) nondairy butter, melted

¼ cup (88 g) molasses

1 teaspoon oil

YIELD: 8 BUNS

In a small bowl, stir the yeast and sugar into the ¼ cup (60 ml)
warm water. Let sit for 10 minutes, until foamy.

In a large mixing bowl, combine the flour, baking soda, baking
powder, and salt.

In a separate bowl, combine the yeast mixture, soymilk, butter,
and molasses.

Add the wet ingredients to the dry and knead until a soft,
elastic dough is formed, adding more water, 1 tablespoon
(15 ml) at a time, if needed.

Knead for about 10 minutes. Form into a ball.

Coat very lightly with the oil and cover with plastic wrap. Let
rise for 45 minutes to 1 hour.

Preheat the oven to 425°F (220°C, or gas mark 7). Line a baking
sheet with parchment or a silicone baking mat.

Punch down the dough and divide into 8 pieces, roll into balls,
and flatten into a bun shape. Place on the prepared baking
sheet and let sit for about 10 minutes.

Bake for 12 to 14 minutes, or until just beginning to brown.

SWEET POTATO BUNS

Nut Free

No-Oil Added

These soft and slightly sweet buns take potato rolls to a whole new level and remind us of why we make our own bread. These soft rolls work well on almost any burger, especially the Masa Masala Burger (page 149).

---

1 large sweet potato or yam

½ ounce (14 g) active dry yeast

2 teaspoons sugar

½ cup (120 ml) warm water

¼ cup (56 g) nondairy butter, melted, plus more for brushing

1 cup (235 ml) soymilk

2 tablespoons (42 g) agave nectar

4 cups (500 g) all-purpose flour, plus more if needed

1 teaspoon salt

———————

YIELD: 12 BUNS

Bring a pot of lightly salted water to a boil.

Peel and cut the sweet potato into chunks and boil until mushy. Meanwhile, stir the yeast and sugar into the warm water. Let sit for 10 minutes, or until doubled in size.

Drain the potatoes. Return to the pot, and mash.

Add the ¼ cup (56 g) butter, soymilk, and agave nectar. Mash until very, very smooth, with as few lumps as possible.

In a separate, large mixing bowl, combine the 4 cups (500 g) flour and salt. Add the yeast mixture to the flour and salt and stir to combine. Add the potato mixture and knead for 8 to 10 minutes, adding more flour if the dough is too sticky.

Knead until a soft, elastic dough ball forms. (I knead it right in the bowl.)

Cover loosely with a dish towel, and let rise for 1 hour.

Preheat the oven to 350°F (180°C, or gas mark 4). Line 2 baking sheets with parchment or a silicone baking mat.

Punch down the dough and knead for about 2 minutes. Add a little more flour if the dough is too sticky.

Divide into 12 equal pieces, roll into balls, and flatten slightly. Place 6 on each baking sheet.

Bake for 12 to 15 minutes.

Remove from the oven, brush with extra melted butter, and bake for 5 minutes longer, or until golden brown on top.

BAGEL BUNS

Nut Free

Soy-Free

Shiny bagel buns are a great way to serve up your breakfast burgers! If you'd like, add poppy seeds, sesame seeds, or—my favorite—everything (garlic, poppy seeds, and coarse sea salt) to your bagels after you boil them but before you bake them by placing them face down in a shallow dish of seeds and then baking face up, and then flipping as directed below.

¼ ounce (7 g) active dry yeast

1 tablespoon (12 g) sugar

1 cup (235 ml) plus ¼ to ½ cup (60 to 120 ml) warm water, divided

4 cups (500 g) all-purpose flour

1½ teaspoons salt

1 tablespoon (15 ml) mild-flavored vegetable oil, plus additional oil for coating

---

YIELD: 8 BAGELS

Stir the yeast and sugar into 1 cup (235 ml) warm water and let sit for 10 minutes.

In a mixing bowl, combine the flour and salt.

Add the yeast mixture and oil. Knead for about 10 minutes, adding more of the remaining water, 2 tablespoons (30 ml) at a time, until you get a smooth, elastic dough ball.

Lightly coat with the vegetable oil, cover with plastic wrap, and let rise for 1 hour.

Punch down the dough. Knead for 2 to 3 minutes.

Divide the dough into 8 equal pieces. Roll into a ball and flatten each ball into a bun shape.

Once again, lightly coat with oil, cover, and let rest for 20 minutes.

Meanwhile, bring a large pot of water to a boil and preheat the oven to 425°F (220°C, or gas mark 7). Line a baking sheet with parchment or a silicone baking mat.

Add 2 or 3 bagel buns to the boiling water and boil for 1 minute, flip over, and boil for 1 minute longer.

Remove from the water with a slotted spoon, let dry for about 1 minute, and place on the prepared baking sheet. Repeat until all 8 bagels have been boiled.

Bake the bagels for 10 minutes, remove from the oven, flip, and bake 10 minutes longer.

AGAVE WHEAT BUNS

Nut Free

Sweet and soft wheat buns for all of your burger needs. They go especially great with the Scarborough Fair Tofu Burger (page 72) and the Earth Burger (page 98).

½ ounce (14 g) quick-rise yeast

1½ cups (188 g) all-purpose flour, plus more as needed

1½ cups (180 g) whole wheat flour

1 teaspoon salt

½ cup (120 ml) nondairy milk

¼ cup (84 g) agave nectar

¼ cup (56 g) nondairy butter, melted

½ cup (120 ml) water

YIELD: 8 BUNS

In a large mixing bowl, combine the yeast, 1½ cups (188 g) all-purpose flour, the whole wheat flour, and the salt.

In a microwave-safe bowl, combine the milk, agave, butter, and water. Warm in the microwave to 110° to 120°F (43° to 48°C), about 1 minute. This step is necessary to activate the yeast.

Slowly add the wet ingredients to the dry and knead into a soft, elastic dough. If your dough is too sticky, add more flour, 1 tablespoon (8 g) at a time. Cover the dough with a dish towel and let sit for 10 minutes. You probably won't see a noticeable rise here, but that's okay.

Line a baking sheet with parchment or a silicone mat.

Punch down the dough, and break into 8 equal pieces. Form into bun shapes, place on the prepared baking sheet, cover with a dish towel, and let rise for about 45 minutes, or until doubled in size.

Preheat the oven to 350°F (180°C, or gas mark 4).

Bake for about 25 minutes, or until golden brown.

Chapter 14

FRIES AND SIDES

Golden, crispy potatoes and other tasty tidbits to complete the meal.

SMOKY POTATO WEDGES

These smoky potato wedges are addicting!

FOR THE SWEET & SMOKY SEASONING:

2 tablespoons (16 g) potato starch

1 tablespoon (14 g) tightly packed brown sugar

½ teaspoon smoked salt

¼ teaspoon garlic powder

¼ teaspoon onion powder

¼ teaspoon smoked paprika

¼ teaspoon black pepper

FOR THE POTATO WEDGES:

4 large russet potatoes

2 tablespoons (30 ml) mild-flavored vegetable oil

2 tablespoons (30 ml) apple cider vinegar

1 teaspoon liquid smoke

To make the seasoning: Add all ingredients to a spice grinder (or a clean coffee grinder, or very dry blender) and grind into a fine powder. Set aside.

Preheat oven to 425°F (220°C, or gas mark 7). Have ready a baking sheet lined with parchment.

To make the potato wedges: Cut each potato into 8 to 12 wedges, depending on desired thickness. Rinse the potatoes under cool water and pat dry.

Add oil, vinegar, and liquid smoke to a large bowl. Add wedges and toss to coat. Add seasoning to bowl and toss to evenly coat.

Arrange wedges in a single layer and bake for 45 to 50 minutes, flipping halfway through. Serve hot.

YIELD: 4 SERVINGS

BAKED SWEET POTATO FRIES

These fries would pretty much go fantastically with any recipe in this book, though one of my favorite pairings is the Edamame Burger on page 144.

1 large or 2 small yams or sweet potatoes

Salt and pepper

Olive oil, for drizzling

YIELD: 2 TO 4 SERVINGS

Preheat the oven to 350°F (180°C, or gas mark 4). Line a baking sheet with foil. Line a plate with paper towels. Wash and pat dry the potatoes. I leave the skin on, but if you prefer, peel them. Cut the potatoes into fry shapes: wedges, steak fries, skinny fries . . . it's totally a personal preference. Arrange the fries on the prepared baking sheet. Sprinkle with salt and pepper to taste, and liberally drizzle with olive oil.

Bake for 20 minutes, then rotate them on the baking sheet and bake for 20 minutes longer.

Transfer to the plate to absorb excess oil.

FRIED ZUCCHINI

Nut Free

Soy-Free

No-Sugar Added

I find it absolutely meditative and sexy to stand in the kitchen and hand chop vegetables. There is a sensuality to it that is simply unexplainable. First the washing and the drying of freshly bought produce, and then the power of the sharp blade slicing and dicing it into little pieces of goodness that will make the meal.

One evening I was very ready to hand slice some zucchini and even got out a hand grater to shred some for burgers, but for some reason, I wanted to try out the slicing attachment on my food processor. I had had the thing for more than two years and had never used that attachment. So I used it. Dang if it didn't slice that zucchini into a bajillion little discs in a matter of 3 seconds! Whoa.

I might just have to use it a little more often . . . seriously, what could be sexier than power tools?

---

2 or 3 zucchini, sliced into rounds

1 cup (125 g) all-purpose flour

½ teaspoon paprika

½ teaspoon cayenne pepper

½ teaspoon dried parsley

Salt and pepper

Oil, for frying

YIELD: 4 SERVINGS

Place the zukes, flour, paprika, cayenne, parsley, and salt and pepper to taste in a large zipper-seal bag and shake until you get a nice coating on each piece. Line a plate with paper towels.

Preheat ¼ inch (6 mm) oil in a cast-iron skillet over high heat. The oil is ready when a piece of dough dropped into it sizzles immediately. Fry these puppies until golden, 1 to 2 minutes per side. Make sure you don't overcrowd the pan.

Remove from the oil with a slotted spoon and transfer to the plate to absorb excess oil.

Pop 'em back into the bag for a fresh coating of the flour mixture.

Meanwhile, add a little bit more oil to the pan and let it heat back up. Then, for the second fry. This time, cook a little longer on each side, to get that yummy golden brown color. After the second fry, it's back to the draining plate.

Serve with Chunky Marinara (page 194) for dipping.

BUFFALO CAULI-TOTS

Nut Free

Gluten-Free

Don't worry, there's still some potato in these tots. . . . . I just replaced half of the potatoes with riced cauliflower to give these little nuggets of crunchy goodness some extra nutrition, you know, since we are going to be dousing them in buttery buffalo sauce.

2 medium Russet potatoes

1½ cups (150 g) riced cauliflower

¼ cup (56 g) nondairy butter, melted, divided

¼ cup (60 ml) of your favorite hot sauce (true to tradition, I use Frank's brand), divided

———

YIELD: 4 SERVINGS

Bring a pot of lightly salted water to a boil. Peel and rinse the potatoes, and boil for 15 to 20 minutes. At this point, they should still be somewhat firm. Drain and rinse cool enough to handle.

Shred the potatoes into a bowl using the coarse section of a hand grater.

Add cauliflower, 2 tablespoons (28 g) of the melted butter, and 2 tablespoons (30 ml) of the hot sauce, and mix until well combined.

Preheat oven to 425°F (220°C). Have ready a baking sheet lined with parchment or a reusable silicone baking mat.

Using a very small ice cream scoop (if you don't have one, you can use a measuring spoon or melon baller) create balls of the mixture, about 2 teaspoons to 1 tablespoon (15 g) of mixture, and arrange in a single layer on the baking sheet. If you are a tot purist, you can hand-form these into cylinder shapes.

Bake for 30 minutes, tossing halfway through, until browned and crispy.

While baking, mix together remaining butter with the remaining hot sauce.

Remove from oven, and carefully transfer to a bowl. Add buffalo mixture to the bowl and toss to coat.

Serve hot.

DILL PICKLE POTATO SMASHERS

Nut Free   Gluten-Free

No-Sugar Added

Have you heard? Dill pickle-flavored everything is all the rage these days. Everything from popsicles, to candy canes! My fav? Dill pickle potato chips. These potato smashers are kind of inspired by them, but not fried and crispy . . . rather baked and creamy with that salty vinegar punch. Fun!

2 pounds (908 g) baby red potatoes, with skin on

1 tablespoon (18 g) coarse sea salt

2 tablespoons (28 g) nondairy butter

2 tablespoons (30 ml) olive oil

2 tablespoons (30 ml) white vinegar

2 tablespoons (13 g) chopped fresh chives, optional

2 teaspoons dried dill, or 2 tablespoons (7 g) fresh chopped dill

Additional salt and pepper, to taste

YIELD: 4 SERVINGS

Preheat oven to 450°F (230°C, or gas mark 8). Line a baking sheet with parchment or a silicone baking mat.

Add potatoes and coarse salt to a medium pot. Cover with water and bring to a boil. Reduce heat and simmer until potatoes are fork tender, about 20 minutes.

Drain and return the potatoes to the pot. Add butter and gently toss to coat.

Arrange the potatoes in a single layer on the baking sheet. Smash each potato into a disc about ½ inch (1.3 cm) thick using a potato masher or the bottom of a heavy bottomed drinking glass.

Bake for 20 minutes. Remove from oven and flip. Drizzle with olive oil and bake for an additional 20 minutes.

Remove from oven and immediately sprinkle with vinegar, chopped chives, dill, and salt and pepper. Serve hot.

GARLIC ROSEMARY FRIES

Nut Free Gluten-Free No-Sugar Added Soy-Free

French fries are a natural go-to side for burgers. The trick to making crispy-on-the-outside-pillowy-soft-on-the-inside fries is the double fry. Most folks don't realize fries have to be fried—not once, but twice! If you have a deep fryer, now is a perfect time to use it. If not, a heavy pot filled with 4 to 5 inches (10 to 12 cm) of oil, will do the trick just fine. Personally, I like to leave the skin on, but if you prefer them skinless, have at it!

4 large Russet potatoes

Oil, for frying (I personally like canola oil for french fries!)

2 tablespoons (20 g) minced garlic

2 tablespoons (11 g) fresh chopped rosemary

½ teaspoon salt

YIELD: 4 SERVINGS

Cut potatoes into desired fry shape (wedges, steak fries, skinny, fat, etc.) and place in a bowl of cold water to prevent discoloring. Soak for at least 2 hours, or up to overnight in the refrigerator. Drain, rinse, and pat completely dry.

Heat oil to 300°F (150°C). Have ready a large bowl lined with paper towels.

Add fries to the oil (make sure they have enough room to float around freely) and fry for 5 to 7 minutes. This will ensure the fries are cooked all the way through. The fries will be tender at this point, but not browned or crispy.

While fries are frying, in a small bowl mix together garlic, rosemary, and salt.

Carefully remove fries from oil, using a slotted or strainer spoon, and transfer to towel-lined bowl to absorb excess oil.

Turn up the heat to 400°F (204°C). Add fries into the oil and fry until golden and crispy, about 2 minutes. Note that the fries will continue to brown once removed from the oil, so take care not to overcook.

Carefully transfer to towel-lined bowl. Toss quickly to drain off excess oil. Remove towels, but leave the fries in the bowl.

While still hot, sprinkle with seasoning mixture and toss to coat. Serve immediately.

FRIED YUCA WITH GRINGA AJI DIPPING SAUCE

Gluten-Free

Soy-Free

Nut Free

No-Sugar Added

Inspired by Peruvian cuisine, but adapted for easier-to-find peppers, this white-girl version of Aji Verde might just become one of your new favorite condiments. The fried yuca is very similar to potato fries, but a little bit sweeter, though not quite as sweet as sweet potato fries. Yuca root—otherwise known as cassava—is brown and rough on the outside, but crisp and white or yellowish on the inside. The thick woody skin is too thick to be peeled with a potato peeler, so you will need to peel it with a knife. If you have a deep fryer, this is a great way to use it. Otherwise, a deep pot filled with about 4 inches (10 cm) of vegetable oil should do just fine.

FOR THE GRINGA AJI DIPPING SAUCE:

6 fresh jalapeño peppers

2 ounces (56 g) fresh baby spinach leaves

1 ounce (28 g) fresh parsley

1 ½ cups (355 ml) mild- flavored vegetable oil oil

2 tablespoons (30 g) minced garlic (about 6 cloves)

1 tablespoon (15 ml) lemon juice

Salt and pepper, to taste

FOR THE FRIED YUCA:

1 large yuca root

½ teaspoon cumin

½ teaspoon salt

½ teaspoon paprika

½ teaspoon garlic powder

½ teaspoon onion powder

Oil, for frying

To make the dipping sauce: Remove the stems from the jalapeños (and seeds, if not using) and place on a lined baking sheet and roast at 350°F (180°C, or gas mark 4) for about 30 minutes.

Add all remaining sauce ingredients to a blender and purée until smooth. Refrigerate until ready to serve.

To make the fried yuca: Peel and slice the yuca into fry-size pieces. Rinse under cool water to remove excess starch and prevent discoloring. Steam fries for about 20 minutes prior to frying. This will soften and precook the fries.

While yuca is steaming, prepare the spice mixture by adding all spices to a small container with a tight-fitting lid and shake to mix.

Preheat oil to 350°F (180°C). Have ready a plate or baking sheet lined with paper towels.

Carefully add steamed fries in small batches to the oil, being careful not to overcrowd. Allow to cook for about 3 to 5 minutes, remove from oil and place on paper towel-lined tray to absorb excess oil. Sprinkle with seasoning mixture to taste. Serve hot with the dipping sauce.

YIELD: 4 SERVINGS OF YUCA AND 2 CUPS (470 ML) SAUCE

CRISPY FRIED ONIONS

No-Sugar Added

Slice those onions as thinly as possible for the crispiest of crispy onions! If you have a deep fryer, this is a good time to use it. If not, a pot filled with about 2 to 3 inches (5 to 7.5 cm) of oil will work just fine. Depending on the milk you choose, this recipe can be made soy-free or nut-free.

1 tablespoon (15 ml) lemon juice

1 cup (235 ml) unsweetened nondairy milk

1 large yellow onion, sliced very thin

Oil, for frying

⅔ cup (84 g) all-purpose flour

¼ teaspoon salt

¼ teaspoon pepper

—————————

YIELD: VARIES DEPENDING ON THE SIZE OF YOUR ONION

Combine lemon juice and unsweetened nondairy milk in a bowl. Set aside for 2 to 3 minutes. It will curdle and become like buttermilk.

Add thinly sliced onions to the buttermilk mixture and let soak for 5 minutes.

Heat oil to 375°F (190°C). Have ready a plate lined with paper towels.

Mix together flour, salt and pepper in a medium bowl. Add in sliced onions and toss to coat.

Carefully add coated onions to the oil, making sure they can float around freely. You may need to do this in several batches. Fry for about 5 minutes, or until golden and crispy all the way through.

Carefully transfer to towel-lined plate to absorb excess oil. Cool completely before storing in an airtight container.

BAKED ONION RINGS

No-Oil Added

No-Sugar Added

Soy-Free

Onion rings come in second only to golden delicious french fries as the perfect side to a burger. And while deep-fried is always delicious, this baked version is darned tasty, too!

1 medium yellow onion, cut into ¼-inch (6- mm) thick slices

⅓ cup (80 ml) aquafaba (liquid from a can of chickpeas)

¼ cup (60 ml) unsweetened almond or other nondairy milk

½ cup (40 g) panko-style bread crumbs

1 teaspoon dried parsley

½ cup (62 g) all-purpose flour

¼ teaspoon smoked paprika

¼ teaspoon salt

⅛ teaspoon black pepper

YIELD: 2 TO 4 SERVINGS

Preheat oven to 450°F (230°C, or gas mark 8). Have ready a baking sheet lined with parchment or a reusable baking mat.

Separate onion slices into individual rings.

In a small bowl, whisk together aquafaba and milk. Set aside.

In a separate bowl, combine panko crumbs and dried parsley. Set aside.

Add flour, paprika, salt, and black pepper to a large resealable plastic bag or a container with a tight-fitting lid. Add onion rings, and shake until they are well coated with flour.

Place flour-coated onion rings into the aquafaba mixture, a few at a time, and toss lightly with tongs until coated.

Transfer to the panko crumbs and toss to coat. Arrange in a single layer on the baking sheet and bake 12 to 15 minutes, or until crumbs are a light golden brown.

GREEN BEAN FRIES

Green beans are good, but FRIED green beans are better!

Oil, for frying

1¼ cups (156 g) all-purpose flour

1 tablespoon (8 g) black sesame seeds

¼ teaspoon baking powder

¼ teaspoon baking soda

1 cup (235 ml) club soda

1 tablespoon (15 ml) toasted sesame oil

½ pound (227 g) fresh green beans, ends trimmed

Heat oil to 350°F (180°C). Have ready a plate lined with paper towels.

In a medium bowl, mix together the flour, sesame seeds, baking powder, and baking soda.

Add the club soda and sesame oil. Mix until just combined and still lumpy. Take care not to overmix.

Coat the green beans in the batter and fry, a few at a time, until the batter is golden and crispy, about 1 minute. Transfer to the paper towel-lined plate to absorb excess oil. Serve immediately.

YIELD: 2 TO 4 SERVINGS

TOTCHOS

Nachos are great, but Totchos are what you want with a burger. These are topped with baked potato toppings. This recipe is family size. Make it in a casserole for the whole gang to munch on. Oh, so you think tater tots are passé? Swap out the tots for Smoky Potato Wedges (page 216).

2 pounds (908 g) frozen tater tots

1 recipe Cheezy Sauce (page 183)

1 cup (100 g) Imitation Bacon Bits, store-bought or homemade (page 201)

½ cup (120 g) nondairy sour cream, store-bought or homemade (page 198)

½ cup (50 g) chopped green onions

Preheat oven to 450°F (230°C, or gas mark 8). Have ready a 3 x 9 x 2-inch (7.5 x 23 x 5 cm) baking dish or casserole dish.

Arrange tots in a single layer and bake 28 to 32 minutes, tossing halfway through, or until golden brown and crisp. Carefully remove from oven. (You can also opt to cook these in a deep fryer for an even more restaurant-style tot.)

Ladle the cheezy sauce all over the top. Sprinkle evenly with bacon bits. Drop dollops of sour cream all over. Sprinkle on the green onions. Serve immediately.

YIELD: 8 SERVINGS

FRIED DILL PICKLES

Soy-Free   Nut Free   No-Sugar Added

Fried pickles? Yes please! But you don't have to limit yourself to pickles. All sorts of veggies taste great dipped in this batter and fried until golden and delicious. A deep fryer works well here, but if you don't have one, a pot filled with 4 inches (10 cm) of oil will work just fine.

Oil, for frying

½ cup (70 g) yellow cornmeal

½ cup (62 g) all-purpose flour

½ teaspoon salt

⅛ teaspoon ground black pepper

¼ teaspoon paprika

1 cup (235 ml) vegan pale lager-style beer (check out barnivore.com to check if your favorite beer is vegan)

25 to 30 dill pickle chips, drained and patted dry

—————

YIELD: 25 TO 30 PIECES

Heat oil to 350°F (180°C). Have ready a plate lined with paper towels.

In a medium mixing bowl whisk together cornmeal, flour, salt, pepper, paprika, and beer until smooth. The batter should be like a thin pancake batter. If the batter is too thin, add a bit more flour. Too thick? Add a bit more beer.

Coat each pickle chip with a thick coating of batter and carefully drop into the hot oil. You can add quite a few to the pot at the same time. Just make sure that they all have enough space to float around in the oil freely.

Fry for about 3 minutes, or until golden brown and crispy.

Using a slotted spoon, transfer to the paper towel-lined plate to absorb excess oil.

Repeat until all pickles are used.

CEDAR-SMOKED TOFU AND PASTA SALAD WITH CHIPOTLE ROASTED RED PEPPER DRESSING

This salad not only goes great with burgers, but it also goes fabulously with just about anything!

1 pound (454 g) pasta of your choice

1 pound (454 g) extra-firm smoked tofu (you can buy it already smoked or make your own, see You Are SO Vegan), cut into bite-size chunks

1 cup (224 g) vegan mayonnaise, store-bought or homemade (page 197)

1 teaspoon garlic powder

1 teaspoon onion powder

1 teaspoon chipotle powder

1 teaspoon chili powder

12 ounces (340 g) roasted red peppers, thinly sliced

14 ounces (396 g) spinach, drained if using canned or cut into chiffonade if fresh

Salt and pepper

YIELD: 8 SERVINGS

Cook the pasta in lightly salted water according to package directions.

Drain and let cool. Or cool off the pasta quickly by running under cold water.

In a large bowl, combine the tofu, mayonnaise, garlic powder, onion powder, chipotle powder, chili powder, red peppers, spinach, and salt and pepper to taste.

Add the pasta and toss to combine.

Refrigerate until ready to eat.

You Are SO Vegan!

To make your own smoked tofu, try this very simple technique. First, buy a food-safe cedar plank. Soak it in water for at least 1 hour, more if you have time. Preheat the oven to 200°F (100°C, or gas mark ¼). Slice a block of extra-firm tofu and arrange on the plank. Place the plank in the oven and bake for 90 minutes to 3 hours. The outside of the tofu will turn brown and become firm. The inside will stay moist and chewy. Use the tofu in any recipe.

CREAMY BBQ COLESLAW

This coleslaw adds a tangy, sassy twist to the classic coleslaw. This tastes great piled onto the Pulled "Pork" Slider (page 182) or on its own as a side dish.

1 cup (224 g) vegan mayonnaise, store-bought or homemade (page 197)

⅓ cup (80 ml) barbecue sauce, store-bought or homemade (page 189)

⅓ cup (116 g) agave nectar

2 tablespoons (30 ml) apple cider vinegar

Salt and pepper

1 medium head cabbage, cored and shredded

In a large bowl, combine the mayonnaise, barbecue sauce, agave, vinegar, and salt and pepper to taste. Add the cabbage and toss to coat.

Refrigerate until ready to serve.

YIELD: 12 SERVINGS

CILANTRO LIME RICE

No-Sugar Added   Gluten-Free   Nut Free

This is my version of the rice they make at Chipotle Mexican Grill. This is another great side dish to serve up alongside the Mexican-inspired burgers, like Sarah's Southwest Burger on page 90.

2 tablespoons (28 g) nondairy butter

1⅓ cups (253 g) uncooked basmati rice

2 cups (470 ml) water

1 teaspoon salt

Juice of 2 limes

¼ cup (4 g) finely chopped fresh cilantro

YIELD: ABOUT 3 CUPS (495 G)

In a pot with a tight-fitting lid, melt the butter over low heat.

Add the rice, and stir to coat. Cook for about 1 minute to lightly toast the rice.

Add the water, salt, and lime juice. Bring to a boil. Reduce to a simmer and cover.

Simmer, covered, for 20 to 25 minutes, or until the rice is tender and the liquid is absorbed. Stir occasionally to prevent the rice from sticking or scorching on the bottom of the pan.

Fluff with a fork and fold in the chopped cilantro.

MEDITERRANEAN ORZO SALAD

Nut Free

No-Sugar Added

This pasta salad is light and tasty without being weighed down in a heavy mayo-based dressing. If you don't have any spinach on hand, any sort of leafy green will work out just fine.

1 pound (454 g) orzo, cooked in salted water according to package directions

14 ounces (396 g) extra-firm tofu, drained, pressed, and cubed

¼ cup (60 ml) olive oil

12 sun-dried tomatoes, chopped

2 cups (60 g) fresh spinach, cut into chiffonade

2 cloves garlic, finely diced

1 tablespoon (8 g) onion powder

12 large leaves fresh basil, cut into chiffonade

12 kalamata olives, pitted and chopped

Salt and pepper, to taste

_____

YIELD: 4 TO 6 SERVINGS

Combine all the ingredients and mix well.

Serve hot or cold.

Tester Recognition

So much gratitude to the amazing recipe testers that sacrificed their time (and sometimes their ingredients!) to help make sure these burgers were book-worthy.

I will never forget the OG testers! Y'all took a leap of faith over a decade ago when this 'lil lady asked you to try over a hundred different veggie burgers!

Liz Wyman, Tamara Harden, Lisa Coulson, Amanda Somerville, Mary Worrell, Jennifer Shrier, Sheree Brit, Cyndee Lee Rule, Amanda Dickie, Jamie Coble, Michelle Graves, Julie Farson, Karyn Casper, and Melisser Elliott. I love you!

About the Author

I am Joni Marie Newman, self-appointed *QUEEN OF VEGGIE BURGERS*! I've been doing this vegan thing for close to fifteen years now, and the most part, I am still just a regular gal who loves to cook, especially for friends and family. I'm self-taught, and will always be learning.

Besides writing cookbooks, I keep pretty busy: working most days on a family owned thirty acre farm, teaching cooking classes, volunteering and organizing vegan events, recording my podcast *Vegan Road Rants*, and raising awareness about veganism and animal liberation with a pro-intersectional approach through various outreach activities. Oh, and every once in a while, I still put up a blog post over on *justthefood.com*.

I'm finally back home in Long Beach, California. One of the things I love most about living in Southern California is the amazing diversity. In my city of Long Beach, I can find the most amazing food from the farthest reaches of the planet! I can literally find Peruvian, Cambodian, Vietnamese, Ethiopian, Korean, Indian, Mexican, Chinese . . . I can go on for pages . . . cuisine within a 20-minute drive.

I have a love of all foods and flavors and am constantly in awe and inspired by the amazing chefs and their foods from other cultures. I try to bring a lot of those flavor profiles into my own interpretations and twists on foods, with a deep admiration and respect to the creators of the originals.

I live with that delicious husband of mine, Dan-the-Microwave-Man Newman in a cute little home we call our own. It is in this humble abode that I create delicious foods for the world to enjoy. Because, through my food, I help people understand that *it is not necessary to murder or torture another living creature in order to have a tasty supper.*

Special Thanks

Thank you! Thank you! Thank you!

A huge heartfelt thanks to: Amanda Waddell, for once again, taking a chance on a book full of veggie burgers. To Celine Steen and Kate Lewis for the incredible photography. To Laura Klynstra (designer), Nyle Vialet, and Katie Benoit, this book wouldn't exist without your hard work and talent.

To Jackie Sobon for keeping me young, and playing restaurant with me at *JJ's Snack Shack.* To Erin Wysocarski for being the best listener in the whole wide world and driving way too far with me just to get lunch. To Jennifer Shrier, Carrie Kim, and Jamie Riera for Buzzballing it with me in the parking lot and being the bestest besties. I love all you ladies more than you can ever know.

And, finally, my sweet, sweet, sweet Daniel Newman. Love of my life. My partner. My best friend. You keep me grounded when I start to flit away. You believe in me. You support me. You love me. Hey, ba-bay! I love you, too!

Thank you. You folks complete me.

Index